5671

9½ NARROW

ALSO BY PATRICIA MORRISROE

Wide Awake: A Memoir of Insomnia
Mapplethorpe: A Biograaphy

9½ NARROW

My Life in Shoes

Patricia Morrisroe

GOTHAM BOOKS

GOTHAM BOOKS

An imprint of Penguin Random House
375 Hudson Street
New York, New York 10014

Copyright © 2015 by Patricia Morrisroe

Gotham Books and the skyscraper logo are trademarks of Penguin Group (USA) LLC.

Parts of "Love on a Shoestring" previously appeared in *Vogue*.

LIBRARY OF CONGRESS CATALOGING-IN-PUBLICATION DATA
has been applied for.

ISBN 978-1-592-40924-2

Printed in the United States of America
1   3   5   7   9   10   8   6   4   2

Set in Adobe Caslon Pro
Designed by Elke Sigal

For my mother, who could never find shoes that fit
but who got the prince anyway.

Contents

Author's Note

The names of some of the persons included
in this memoir have been changed.

Introduction

 $\mathcal{L}$ ast month I was killing time before a dentist's appointment when I wandered into a "shoe event" at Bergdorf Goodman. Dozens of women were teetering on five-inch heels and drinking champagne. Shoe boxes were everywhere. I spotted a pair of studded black boots that I didn't need and couldn't afford, but after inhaling the scent of shoe lust—a carnal blend of animal hides with a splash of insanity—I flagged the nearest salesperson.

"Is your name on the list?" he asked. A list for what? Boots? But apparently there was a list, and I was not on it. As a consolation prize, he offered me champagne, but I didn't want champagne. I wanted the boots. The salesman seemed genuinely perplexed by my inability to grasp the obvious. The boots were already "pre-sold." Did I actually expect to waltz into the store in early September and come away with a pair of highly coveted fall boots that other customers had been plotting to acquire since the previous spring?

I thanked him and gathered my things while he checked out my bag and shoes.

Sensing that he might be losing a potential customer, he motioned me closer. "Maybe I can do something," he whispered. "I'll see what's in the back room." He zigzagged around the shoe boxes and disappeared. He was gone so long, it gave me plenty of time to wonder if the back room was so far back it was now in New Jersey. When he returned, he was out of breath. "I was saving these for a celebrity," he said, "but she never showed up." The boots were a size 8½. I'd asked for a 9½.

"They run large," he explained, "and I see that you have very narrow feet, so they might fit."

They didn't, although that didn't stop me from parading around in them, hoping they'd conform to my feet through sheer force of will. As I circled the room, I attracted the attention of several tipsy women, who were heading for the escalator with shopping bags filled with shoe boxes. They spotted the boots and began to follow me.

"Unfortunately, they're too short," I told the salesman.

He gave me the name of an elite shoe repair shop that could stretch them.

"And they're too wide."

"I can get you some insoles."

"I'm sorry, but I'm afraid they don't fit."

The women gazed down at my poor pathetic feet, the feet that couldn't fit into the boots a celebrity had almost wanted. I could feel their pity and, it must be said, their disgust. I didn't have a pedicure, which made me the outlier in a room of perfectly painted toenails. I would never get the boots or the prince because in a weird twist on *Cinderella,* my feet were both too slender and too large.

We're living in the Shoe Age, when women have determined that there is nothing more fulfilling, more thrilling than a pair of head-turning, sole-killing "statement" heels. While not a new phenomenon—women have always been shoe-obsessed—we've entered an era when shoes have not only become the most important fashion accessory but also the most profitable item in high-end department stores. Conquering territory that once belonged to designer clothes, shoes are now displayed in the equivalent of footwear museums. In 2007, Saks Fifth Avenue was one of the first to jump on the trend when it turned its eighth floor into a shoe emporium so enormous it needed its own ZIP code—10022-SHOE. Five years later, it felt cramped, so Saks added another 7,000 square feet, including on-site shoe repair. Not to be outdone, Barneys created a 22,000-square-foot shoe department that spanned the whole fifth floor, with Italian marble walls, glass and ebony wood tables, and iPad stations. Macy's, with 63,000 square feet containing nearly 300,000 pairs of shoes, claims to be the largest shoe department in the entire world, but Harrods in London and Lane Crawford in Hong Kong are fast catching up.

Department stores need to do everything they can to entice shoppers, who can easily click on a retail website, such as Net-A-Porter, and have Christian Louboutin's Follies Resille five-inch pumps "crafted from gold leather and glitter-finished fishnet" overnighted to their homes. If their size is sold out, they can go on any number of social commerce websites and locate them in London, Singapore, or Berlin. The e-tailer Yoox started an online shoe store, Shoescribe, after it discovered that sales of shoes far outpaced those of any other items.

Where once viewed as secondary to handbags, shoes are increasingly essential to a designer's brand. In addition to being highly lucrative, they expose new customers to a designer's ready-to-wear business, as well as frequently dictating the look of fashion shows.

When heels go up, hemlines do too; when they go down, dresses become looser, pants slouchier. With prices for designer clothes increasingly out of reach, shoes may feel like a relative bargain, and with clothes becoming more casual, they add an element of sophistication. Shoes are fun to shop for. They don't require you to enter a dressing room and stare at your cellulite under unflattering light. Feet may develop bunions and corns, but they'll never get fat, and they'll still look beautiful—in the right shoes.

Sex and the City brought "shoe porn" to the masses. From 1998 to 2004, Sarah Jessica Parker, as the shoe-obsessed Carrie, introduced TV audiences to such high-end designers as Manolo Blahnik, Jimmy Choo, and Christian Louboutin. "Manolos" became so popular that 37 percent of women surveyed in a *Women's Wear Daily* poll claimed they'd bungee jump off the Golden Gate Bridge in exchange for a lifetime supply of them. In the fall of 2014, Parker introduced her own line of footwear, SJP, which included a strappy spike named the Carrie.

⅋

By the time I reached the dentist's office, I couldn't stop thinking about shoes. For a brief moment, I even thought about Imelda Marcos, who, after fleeing the Philippines with her dictator husband, left a cache of her famous designer high heels behind. Termites invaded the presidential palace and ate them. Then I began thinking about Bernie Madoff, whose possessions were sent to the auction block to help compensate his victims. What captured the public's imagination was not his collection of Patek Philippe watches, or his wife's 10-karat emerald-cut diamond, or the Steinway grand piano, or the cow-shaped creamer. It was the 250 pairs of handmade Belgian loafers in the "Mr. Casual" style. The press had a field day with headlines such as WALK A DAY IN BERNIE MADOFF'S SHOES. Not that any would want to, since he was serving 150 years in prison, but the shoes came to symbolize Madoff's improbable journey from prominent investment advisor to notorious financial swindler.

Marie Antoinette, whose reputation for extravagance earned her the title Madame Déficit, bought shoes by the hundreds. The queen's trip to the guillotine is rife with shoe imagery. During her escape from the storming of the Tuileries Palace, she lost a delicate high-heeled slipper with ruched ribbon trim that is now in the Musée Carnavalet in Paris. She wore two-inch plum-black mules to her beheading. Her final words, "Pardon me, sir, I meant not to do it," were uttered to the executioner after she accidentally stepped on his foot. More recently, the veteran war correspondent Marie Colvin was killed in Syria when she returned to a building to retrieve her shoes during a rocket attack. In keeping with local customs, she'd removed them before entering.

Shoes not only tell stories but are also thought to indicate character. In 2005, Secretary of State Condoleezza Rice toured Wiesbaden Army Airfield in a pair of black stiletto boots that the *Washington Post*'s fashion editor, Robin Givhan, viewed as a refreshing demonstration of power, sex, and toughness. Later that year, Rice was roundly criticized for going shoe shopping at the Fifth Avenue Ferragamo immediately after Hurricane Katrina hit the Gulf Coast. Sarah Palin, in her debut as vice presidential candidate, chose a pair of bright-red, high-heeled Double Dare pumps by Naughty Monkey, a brand that usually caters to twenty-year-old club kids. If Palin was viewed as inappropriately sexy, Representative Michele Bachmann, in her 2012 presidential run, was often photographed in dowdy open-toed orthopedic-style sandals paired with pantyhose. She claimed high heels triggered her migraines, which set off a whole flurry of stories about how she'd deal with the stress of the presidency. Michelle Obama, famous for her chic mix of high and low, wore a pair of relatively affordable J. Crew pumps to the 2013 Inauguration Day festivities. The shoes offset the expensive made-to-order Thom Browne coat, signaling that she was both glamorous and grounded.

Shoes play an important role in fairy tales, largely due to their sexual connotations. To Freud, they symbolized the vagina, with the foot representing male and female castration anxieties. When Cinderella slides her foot into the smooth glass slipper, she is signaling to the prince that they will live happily ever after, at least in the bedroom.

Even in real life, shoes have figured prominently in courtship and marriage rituals. In some countries, the father of the bride presented the groom with his daughter's shoes to symbolize the transfer of authority. When placed on the husband's side of the wedding bed, the bride's shoe signified ownership and fostered fertility. People still tie old shoes to the bumper of a newlywed's car as a way of wishing good luck.

Our language is filled with shoe references. If something is very soothing and familiar, it's as "comforting as an old shoe." If we assume someone else's responsibilities, we're "stepping into his shoes." When we grow fearful, we "wait for the other shoe to drop." When someone experiences a spate of bad luck, we tell ourselves that we "wouldn't want to be in his shoes." In the war against terrorism, we even have a new term: *shoe bomber*.

From crocheted booties to orthopedic brogues, shoes mark important rites of passage, reminding us of both the good and bad times—the road not taken, the prince not caught, the missed opportunities, the dancing, the traveling, the fun. While I can't always recall the dresses or coats I wore on various occasions, I have a vivid memory of the white Mary Janes that represented my first shoe "crush"; the confirmation wedgies that celebrated my entrance to adulthood; the red patent-leather Puma sneakers my husband sported on our first date; the gray ostrich flats I wore to a girlfriend's funeral; the New Balance sneakers I bought my elderly mother, who was losing her balance and was too proud to use a cane.

This is my shoe story, but it could just as easily be yours. So kick off your heels, put up your feet, and for the next few hours, walk with me.

1

White Mary Janes

It was the summer of 1961. Kennedy was in the White House, I was in church, and Hannah Howard was in a pair of white Mary Janes. Hannah was the prettiest girl in my school. She had long platinum hair, bright-blue eyes, and a Hollywood pedigree, a rarity in Andover, Massachusetts, where Harriet Beecher Stowe, author of *Uncle Tom's Cabin*, was the town's biggest celebrity. Hannah's mother was Priscilla Lane, who had starred in dozens of movies, including *The Roaring Twenties*, with James Cagney and Humphrey Bogart, and *Arsenic and Old Lace*, with Cary Grant. Priscilla Lane, by then Mrs. Howard, had also been my Brownie leader and looked so striking in her uniform that I never missed a troop meeting and briefly considered a military career.

Whenever Hannah and Mrs. Howard walked up to the Communion rail, even the most devout churchgoers put down their missals and gawked. I was among the worst offenders. On that particular

Sunday, I kept staring at their outfits as I inched my way toward the altar rail. They were in the line opposite me, so I had an especially good view. Suddenly, I felt a sharp poke in my back. It was my mother, and I knew exactly what the poke meant: *You stop right now! You're in church!* But I couldn't stop because I'd already fallen in love with Hannah's white Mary Janes.

⁂

In hindsight, I realize I was infatuated not so much with the shoes but with the concept of Hollywood perfection viewed through the eyes of a ten-year-old. Though my mother was blond and very pretty, she wasn't a movie star, and nobody would ever mistake me for a movie star's daughter. Instead of long platinum hair, I had a brunette pixie cut that clung to my head like an upside-down artichoke, and I was tall, skinny, and so pale my mother kept pressing me to "get some color." When the neighborhood kids played cowboys and Indians, I was usually cast as the English princess, whose sole responsibility was sitting in a claustrophobic teepee, waiting for the cowboys to rescue me. Usually, they were too busy shooting toy guns and shouting racist comments at the Indians to remember they'd left "Princess Pale Skin" behind.

I couldn't imagine Hannah wasting her precious youth in an overheated teepee. She was probably a regular at Disneyland, where her family received preferential treatment through her mother's Hollywood connections. I knew that envy was a sin, but I wanted to be Hannah Howard. I immediately felt guilty for not thinking more spiritual thoughts, especially with Father Smith holding the Host in front of my face. As I returned to my pew, I tried to extricate the sticky wafer from the roof of my mouth, while praying to be a better person. It was then I experienced an epiphany. While not spiritual or particularly profound, it resonated with me. I couldn't walk in Hannah's shoes, but I could, if my mother agreed, own the same pair.

"*White* shoes?" my mother said as we drove home from church. "Are you crazy? They're going to get filthy and then what will you do?"

"Clean them."

"They'll never look the same. You've had some crazy ideas but *white* shoes, well, that's the craziest. Just you wait. Your father is going to have *plenty* to say about that."

My father worked in finance, first as a bank examiner, and then in the mortgage department at the Arlington Trust Company, where everybody said he was the nicest man they'd ever met. Despite his outgoing personality during business hours, he was a naturally reticent person who treasured his brief moments of privacy. One of his greatest pleasures was reading *The Boston Globe* and the *Lawrence Eagle-Tribune,* which he'd focus on so intensely he seemed to go into a trance. His mother had died when he was four, and since my grandfather, who worked for the Massachusetts Bay Transportation Authority, couldn't take care of seven children, the family was split up. Depending on their ages, some stayed with relatives or were sent away to school. My father and his older brother, Joe, wound up with their aunt, a Dominican nun who lived in a nearby convent. When they turned seven, they attended a strict all-boys Catholic school, where they joined other students who'd been orphaned or whose parents couldn't keep them at home. As a form of survival, my father had learned from an early age that books and newspapers were powerful tools of escape. Raised not to whine or complain, he was stoic to a fault. If anyone ever asked how he was, he'd always give the same answer: "I'm fine."

I knew he wasn't going to have "plenty" to say about my Mary

Janes because he wouldn't waste a syllable on anything as trivial as fashion. This was strictly a mother-daughter issue. My mother told me I had enough shoes and that I was turning into a very greedy little girl, and you know what happens to greedy little girls?

While she painted a very dark picture of my future, we noticed a skunk in our backyard. It had built a den not far from where we played croquet, preventing us from channeling our frustrations through competitive sport. For the next several days, my mother rapped on the kitchen window and screamed, "Get out, you pest!" Sensing no danger whatsoever, the skunk continued to ignore her, and because my mother was afraid it would soon take over the house—she tended to endow animals with human qualities—she called the Andover police. In all fairness, she hadn't expected a firing squad. The policemen explained that skunks are rarely seen in daylight during the summer, unless they have rabies. The skunk had to go. To this day, I can still hear them shouting, "Ready! Aim! Fire!" It was not a clean kill. The skunk staggered around our croquet set, before collapsing, dead, over a wicket.

I became hysterical, and to calm me down, my mother offered to buy me a Popsicle. "I just saw an animal being killed before my very eyes," I cried. "You think a Popsicle is going to make that image go away?"

"Then what would?"

I pretended to think for a few seconds. "Hmmm," I said. "White Mary Janes?"

⁂

A few hours later, with my new shoes and a celebratory Popsicle, my mother told me I should be grateful to the skunk, whose death had not been in vain, though the animal did blanket the neighborhood with a noxious odor. It was a small price to pay for such beautiful shoes. As I was admiring the way the white leather blended seamlessly with my white legs, my mother casually dropped a bombshell: "You were born with twelve toes, you know." Before I had time to process this bizarre piece of information, she ran into the kitchen to answer the telephone. The street was abuzz with rumors that she'd killed someone.

Twelve toes? Where did that come from? While I could understand her calling me the prettiest baby in the hospital nursery—except for a boy with an unusually large head, I was the only baby—but twelve toes? That's not something mothers usually brag about unless they live in parts of Asia, where extra digits are considered good luck, but in Andover, twelve toes aren't necessarily bad luck. They're just not a big advantage.

Simple things like nursery rhymes suddenly become darker and more complex. What's a mother to do after the fifth little piggy goes "wee wee wee" all the way home, and she's stuck with a sixth little piggy? Does she send it off to market again? Pretend it's a Siamese twin? And what happens when the baby gets older and learns that 5 + 1 doesn't equal 5½ or, if the mother is in total denial, 5?

I came home from the hospital minus two, so I was spared the math problems, but the story, as I soon discovered, didn't add up.

"So, about those twelve toes," I said when she returned from explaining to the elderly woman next door why her rhubarb smelled "off."

"What are you talking about?" my mother replied. "I never said you had twelve toes. What I said, if you'd listened carefully, is that you were born with jaundice."

My mother was a master at blurting out things and then developing temporary amnesia.

I was pretty sure that I hadn't confused a condition that causes yellow skin with a birth defect that results in extra digits. Even if my mother had used the medical term for jaundice, which is *icterus*, it still sounded nothing like *twelve toes*. I took a closer look at my little toes. Why did they have identical scars? "Corns," my mother said. "We all get them." But babies don't walk far enough to develop corns. They take a few steps and then go boom to the kind of wild applause they'll probably never hear again in their entire lives.

The sudden revelation of my missing toes brought out the inner detective in me. I was a major fan of Nancy Drew books, which my mother bought for me the minute a new one came out. My mother read them too, though she made me promise never to tell anyone. "I'm just a kid at heart," she'd say.

Whenever my mother slathered herself with baby oil and went outside to "work" on her tan—most women treated tanning as an actual job—I attempted to solve *The Mystery of the Twelve Toes*. My first stop was the family photo album, which my father had started when I was born and kept up regularly throughout the years. It sat on the bottom shelf of the living room bookcase, wedged between Ernie Pyle's *Here Is Your War* and Alexandre Dumas's *The Count of Monte Cristo*.

With an old magnifying glass I'd discovered in the basement, I immediately struck gold. A photo marked *First Day Home from Hospital* showed me kicking up my bare feet on my parents' bed. My mother's index finger extended into the frame, pointing at my left little toe. Using the magnifying glass, I began counting. One, two, three . . . *ten*. If two were removed, why didn't I have bandages? And who cut off the toes? The obstetrician? A nearsighted mohel?

Right then, I had an image of dancing feet, and I recalled with some repulsion Hans Christian Andersen's fairy tale *The Red Shoes*.

It's the story of a little girl who receives a pair of beautiful red dancing slippers that she can't stop thinking about even during church service. The shoes eventually take over her life, forcing her to dance until her feet bleed. She can't remove them, so she visits the local executioner and asks him to chop off her feet.

"You cried when you read that," my mother recalled. A gigantic cumulus cloud had settled over the backyard, and she had come indoors for some iced tea and to check on the progress of her "color."

"Gee, I wonder why?" I said. "The girl winds up with two stumps for feet and then dies in the end."

"But she goes to heaven."

"So you think I'm like that vain little girl and as punishment I imagined that someone chopped off my toes."

"I'm not saying that exactly. But didn't this toe obsession of yours start with those white Mary Janes?"

2

The Dog Ate My Mules

Reinhold's Shoe Store on Main Street was my favorite place in town. It had a vending machine that dispensed brightly colored gumballs, and another packed with exotic trinkets, such as mini trolls, rubber spiders, and rings that glowed in the dark. Its biggest attraction was a strange-looking wooden cabinet that my mother warned me never to touch because it might explode. It was called a shoe-fitting fluoroscope, and until the early 1950s, it could be found in 10,000 shoe stores across the United States.

The machine used X-rays to take pictures of a person's foot inside a new pair of shoes, allowing the salesmen to see the bones and soft tissue. Though the method was deemed essential for a "scientific fit," customers were exposed to twice the recommended dose of radiation every time they placed their feet directly on the X-ray tube. After people began to worry that tight shoes were less of a problem than radiation-induced cancer, the fluoroscope was phased out.

Reinhold's kept theirs as a reminder that "fitting" shoes was more important than "selling" them, and to that end, the salesmen were never without their Brannock Devices. Named after inventor Charles Brannock, it's an aluminum contraption that you rarely see in adult shoe stores and never in high-end ones, where fashion trumps fit. This would have broken Brannock's heart. The child of a shoe store owner, he'd become obsessed with creating an accurate foot-measuring device in the mid-1920s while a student at Syracuse University. His hobby made him somewhat of an oddity at Delta Kappa Epsilon, where he kept his frat brothers up nights making a prototype from an Erector set, but the Brannock Device eventually became the standard measurement tool.

The concept of measurement was based originally on the foot, which sounds so obvious, until you realize we're talking about the actual human foot. With limited tools at their disposal, our ancestors used whatever was "handy," including, of course, their hands. The human foot was roughly twelve inches, so a foot equaled—twelve inches. According to the Anglo-Saxons, an inch was three barleycorns, and a quarter of a barleycorn was a poppy seed. In both the United States and the United Kingdom, this antiquated method is still the basis of shoe size today. At my current size, I'm twenty-seven barleycorns and six poppy seeds, or 9½.

Prior to the Brannock Device, feet were measured with a simple measuring stick that focused purely on length. Brannock introduced the radical idea of width, from AAA to EEE. I was a triple A. The salesmen always complimented me on my slender feet, not realizing they might have been a whole lot wider with two extra toes. But no matter the size or configuration, Reinhold's had something for everyone. After carefully measuring each foot, one of the bland-looking salesmen—they all wore variations of beige and brown—would disappear into the storage room, climbing a ladder to reach the top shelves. Five or ten minutes later, he'd emerge with so many boxes you couldn't see his face. Like Prince Charming, he'd kneel down in front of you, take your foot in his hand, and with a long metal shoe-horn, he'd slip on the first of a dozen selections. Out of boredom or bad taste, he'd occasionally come back with something totally inappropriate, such as the silver lamé marabou mules that he claimed were the "latest thing for the boudoir." My mother, who'd been chatting with a friend near the fluoroscope, glanced over as I paraded up and down in the backless high heels. "Take those off immediately!" she said. "They look ridiculous!" The salesman quickly shoved them back in the box and disappeared into the stockroom.

My mother was a stickler about quality at a good price, and in those days, that meant only one brand: Stride Rite. In 1919, the company started out in a converted stable in Boston, not far from the city of Lynn, which was then the shoe capital of the world. While the wealthiest women went to Europe for custom-made shoes, companies in the United States, catering to a large and diverse population, were forced to offer multiple sizes, colors, and styles that weren't available from European mass-marketing companies. As a result, America owned the ready-to-wear shoe business until the 1950s, when shoe manufacturing, like other industries such as wool processing, were caught in the post–World War II industrial decline. By the 1970s, highly respected firms such as Delman and I. Miller, which had hired Andy Warhol to do its shoe illustrations, fell into bankruptcy.

Whenever my mother bought a pair of shoes for me, she sometimes bought a pair for herself, but she'd usually return them. Despite the Brannock Device and the ministrations of the very attentive salesmen, the shoes never fit once she got home. Her feet were totally normal too—a size 8B. I could never figure it out. She'd get frustrated and say, "Dear Lord, help me," and then go back to Reinhold's. I think she missed the fluoroscope. There was something comforting about knowing the salesman could see the skeleton of her foot inside her shoes. Without that, she had to rely on her own intuition, and when it came to her feet, it consistently let her down.

"At least *you* got shoes," she'd say. My mother was competitive as well as indecisive, which usually gave me the edge. I was an only child for nearly seven years and my father's job as a bank examiner kept him on the road much of the week. As a result, my mother and I spent a lot of quality time in front of our new Magnavox TV. Since she didn't like to cook, we ate Swanson TV dinners on special TV trays while watching *Father Knows Best* or *Lassie*. We usually wore lounging pajamas, which we didn't wear to bed because they were only for TV viewing. To up the glamour quotient, I suggested to my mother that she might want to buy the silver mules since they matched the aluminum TV dinners, but she was distracted by the blizzard in our Magnavox. Even before global warming, it "snowed" in the weirdest places, such as inside Mrs. Cleaver's kitchen or Lassie's farmhouse. When that happened, you had two options: You could either wait for the weather to pass or fiddle with the rabbit ears, a delicate operation that required a sure hand and a gentle touch.

"Darn it," my mother said. "It's still snowing. Now we'll never find out if Lassie is going to rescue that little boy stuck in the mine."

Even though I was thirty years younger and considerably less worldly, blizzard or no blizzard, I had a strong hunch that Lassie would rescue the adorable kid. Patience, however, wasn't my mother's strongest virtue. Neither was TV repair. Getting up to fix the picture, she yanked the rabbit ears so hard one of them broke off. She blamed me for bringing up the mules when I should have been focus-

ing on Lassie. Now I'd wrecked the TV and we'd probably get electrocuted. "You better turn it off," she said. "I'm afraid."

Sometimes my mother was so impossible I felt like tearing out my
hair, but with my pixie cut, I didn't have a lot to spare. "It's your
fault," I said. "You don't even know how to work rabbit ears."

"I do too."

"Do not."

⁂

Our rivalry intensified when my widowed maternal grandfather came
to live with us. "Bumpa" was a very special person with a high tolerance for bickering. He also suffered from tinnitus and had trouble
hearing. Bumpa was an excellent cook, a skill he learned somewhere
along his versatile career that included being a merchant marine, a
butler, an opera singer, and a music teacher at the Brooks School, in
North Andover. With my father starting his new job at the Arlington
Trust Company and my mother giving birth to my sister Emily, we
were now officially "a family." Which meant no more TV dinners.

In addition to his cooking skills and various other talents, Bumpa
was a master storyteller. Though born in Ireland, he'd long ago
dropped his telltale accent for one that made him sound like John
Gielgud in *Hamlet*. The bottom drawer of his bureau was devoted to
his "memorabilia," which included pictures of exotic-looking women
he encountered prior to his marriage to my English grandmother.
"Who's this?" I asked about a dark-skinned woman with a head scarf
and hoop earrings. "Oh, just a gypsy who lived in the next village,"
he said. Apparently she "read" the back of people's feet instead of
their palms, and then, for an extra fee, she'd throw in a foot rub. "I
learned the technique at her feet," he joked.

Bumpa was a brilliant masseur and my mother and I fought constantly over which of us would gain his attention. After dinner my mother would say, "Dad, my feet are killing me," and then I'd say, "My feet are killing *me*," and soon we'd be demonstrating whose feet were killing them more by limping around like Tiny Tim. Out of deference to her seniority and acting skills, Bumpa usually let my mother go first.

I kept a close watch on the clock, and after the allotted fifteen minutes, I'd say, "Time's up," and then it would be my turn. My mother claimed that Bumpa had "healing hands," which made it sound as if he could cure the lame. He used a special green liniment from the local barbershop. It contained menthol and peppermint and made your feet tingle for hours. Sometimes my feet tingled so much I couldn't fall asleep, and then I'd request a nonmentholated food massage just to calm my nerves.

Bumpa kept the liniment in his closet next to the wooden foot roller he used to strengthen his arches and maintain flexibility. He was religious about his "daily constitutional," which could last for hours, especially when a neighbor invited him in for tea. He'd tell stories to anyone—the newspaper boy, the garbage man, the guy who sprayed weed killer on the lawn. If the subject of opera happened to come up during a discussion of trash or herbicides, he might even sing a few bars from *La Bohème*. This embarrassed my mother no end. "Dad, just stop it!" she'd say. "He's here for the dandelion spores, not a concert." Bumpa had a sweet temperament, so he'd never get angry, though occasionally he'd mutter, "Just take me out feetfirst." He was referring to the old wives' tale about the importance of carrying the dead body out of the house with the head facing away. Otherwise, the spirit would look back and beckon another family member to the grave. Bumpa was full of superstitions, although he'd never heard the one about extra toes bringing good luck. Then again, he'd never heard about my extra toes.

"Who told you that?" he asked.

"Mommy," I said.

"Then it must be true."

After I explained that she'd subsequently denied it, he said, "Then I guess it's not true."

"What's true—the extra toes? Or no extra toes?" Now I was getting exasperated.

He heaved a big sigh. "Just take me out feetfirst."

One day, my mother came home with a pair of marabou mules. She'd returned a sensible tie shoe that was too tight across the instep, and the salesman convinced her that maybe she'd have better luck with something a little less rigid, something "for the boudoir." Since our lounging days were behind us, I felt she'd missed the boat on that one, but perhaps she was trying to recapture the glamour of our TV dinner days. She wore the mules a few times, but her feet kept slipping out of them and once she nearly fell down the stairs. "I could have killed myself," she said. "All because of these stupid mules. I'm taking them right back."

That was good news. Whenever she left the house, I'd use the valuable time to snoop through her personal belongings. To my disappointment, she wasn't a woman of mystery, and I didn't find adoption or divorce papers or any evidence of my missing toes. If I'd been Nancy Drew, I was sure I'd have come up with a diary, or a broken locket, or an old copy of *Gray's Anatomy*, with the page turned down on "The Foot."

Nancy and I both had dogs, but as detectives, they were total duds.

Hers was named Togo and, depending on the book, he was a fox or bull terrier. Either way, he was useless. Buff, my cocker spaniel, had a mischievous streak that no one but me found endearing. His favorite pastime was digging up my mother's flower beds. One afternoon, to distract him from the tulips, I let him loose in my parents' bedroom to see if he'd pick up any suspicious scents. Eventually, I went to practice piano and forgot about him. My mother returned home while I was playing Rondo Alla Turca, and I heard a scream from upstairs.

"The dog has something caught in his throat," she yelled. "He's choking to death!"

Had he found the toes? She picked him up and we raced off to the vet's office, while Buff kept making horrible choking noises. My mother was afraid he'd expire in our new white Ford Fairlane. It had a bright-red interior, which really wasn't my parents' style, but my mother didn't have the patience to order a more subdued color from the car dealership. "Now I'll think *blood* every time I get into this car," she said, "and we'll have to go for a trade-in."

"He's not bleeding," I said, wanting to clarify his medical condition. "He's just choking."

"Oh, Miss Smarty-Pants. I guess you're a doctor now."

The vet took us immediately, even though a hamster was next in line. Its tail had been stapled to the cover of a Popeye coloring book, and if I'd had to guess who did it, I'd have picked the boy with the mother who kept saying, "If Hammy dies, you will NEVER get another pet again. Do . . . you . . . hear . . . me?"

"What has he been eating?" the vet asked, prying open Buff's mouth and looking down his throat with a little flashlight. I thought it best to keep the "toe theory" to myself.

With a tiny instrument that looked like tweezers, he pulled something out. "There, I've got it," he said. I closed my eyes.

"What is it?" my mother asked. "It's all sparkly."

I imagined a baby toe with iridescent nail polish.

"It appears to be a feather," the vet says. "Was the dog chasing birds?"

Buff had obviously found my mother's new marabou mules, perhaps mistaking them for an exotic species of tulips.

When we got home, my mother went upstairs to her bedroom and held up the slippers. With the vet's bill, the mules were the most expensive pair of shoes she'd ever owned and now she couldn't even return them. "Without the feathers, they look like any old ordinary pair of slippers," she complained. Actually, they looked worse, because Buff had left teeth marks on the satin.

The next time we went to Reinhold's, the salesman said, "I guess the mules worked out. You didn't bring them back."

Pleased that she could finally give him a positive report, she gushed, "Yes, they were wonderful."

"*Were?*" he said.

"Our dog ate them," I explained.

"It happens," he said, disappearing into the stockroom to get my mother a brand-new pair.

3

The Killer Podiatrist

*W*hen I was young, "sexiness" was equated with bullet-shaped breasts and killer stilettos. *Stiletto* is Italian for "little knife," and during the Renaissance, it was the weapon of choice for assassins, who could easily hide the needle-pointed blade among their robes before inflicting a mortal blow with a single, well-placed thrust. Over the years, stiletto shoes also have been used as murder weapons, although the end result has never been as clean or as swift. In April 2014, a Houston woman murdered her boyfriend by striking him twenty-five times in the head with pair of cobalt-blue stiletto pumps. Though the boyfriend had given her $1,500 Louboutin stilettos, she used her $50 knockoff versions, thereby preserving the resale value of the originals.

Stilettos came into vogue after World War II, when women left their jobs and returned to their traditional roles as wives and mothers. During the war, the U.S. government and Hollywood conspired to create the "pinup girl," distributing glossy photos of Betty Grable and other stars to boost the morale of the boys overseas. In the most iconic photograph, Grable is in a white bathing suit, wearing high heels and flaunting her famous legs. After *Esquire* magazine published a calendar of Alberto Vargas's images of scantily clad women in heels, the pictures were reproduced on the "noses" of military bombers. As a result, high heels became good luck charms, fetish objects, and something ordinary women needed to wear in order to compete with the idealized pinup that helped us win the war.

Many designers had been working on ways to reinforce the fragile stiletto heel with steel pins encased in wood or plastic, but Roger Vivier, Christian Dior's footwear designer, is widely given credit as the shoe's inventor. In 1947, Dior created the New Look, which featured an ultrafeminine silhouette, with opulent full skirts and cinched waists. After the deprivation of the war years, the clothes gave women a way to mitigate the memory of rationing. With materials in short supply, they'd had to wear sensible platforms made of cork or wood. Now they could embrace sexy shoes, and the stiletto, with its slim silhouette, was the perfect complement to the fuller skirts and dresses.

My mother had a pair of black stilettos that she saved for cocktail parties and my father's college alumni functions. She carried a gold mesh bag with a rhinestone clasp, and before leaving the house, she'd spray her neck and wrists with her favorite scent, My Sin by Lanvin. I thought the name very risqué. It came in a black bottle with a gold top, and on the front was a picture of a mother and daughter that was based on a sketch by the French illustrator Paul Iribe. I'd forever associate the perfume with my mother's racy stilettos. After the parties, she'd usually limp into the house with the shoes in her hand. "Never again am I going to wear these things," she'd say, but of course she did. It gave her an extra excuse to see her foot doctor.

⁊

My mother's podiatrist was considered a "lady killer." He looked like George Clooney, but since nobody knew what George Clooney looked like back then, everybody compared him to Cary Grant. Why such a drop-dead gorgeous guy opted to spend his life around bunions and hammertoes was a total mystery. He also gave pedicures. Though he didn't apply polish, he did all the nasty stuff, like treating ingrown toenails and shaving corns.

His office was in a white Victorian house at the end of our street, not far from the center of town—convenient because Andover was in the throes of foot hysteria, an ailment specific to the female population. I don't recall ever seeing a man at the podiatrist's, but men rarely went to doctors unless they were gravely ill. The only ones my father ever saw were members of his Sunday doubles tennis game. Since the doctors are all dead and he's alive, he feels totally vindicated in having kept their relationship to the serve-and-volley kind.

My mother always dressed up for the doctor, wearing her favorite mink poodle pin on a purple tweed jacket. She usually dragged me to the podiatrist's along with the mink poodle, and I'd be stuck in the waiting room with nothing to read but old copies of *Yankee* magazine. I remember one column, "Sayings of the Oracle," which answered readers' boring questions, such as "Why are bridges covered?" and "Why do dogs eat grass?" At least Mrs. Godfrey, my mother's hairdresser, left copies of *Photoplay* and *Silver Screen* in baskets near all three hair dryers so clients could read about the fabulous lives of the stars.

Despite swallowing mouthfuls of gelatin capsules, my mother's toenails didn't grow fast enough to warrant weekly visits, so I was called into service. Orthotics had suddenly become popular owing to the development of lightweight thermoplastics that molded easily to the foot. Up until the 1960s, people who needed extra support had to make do with pieces of laminated leather that were often bulky and uncomfortable. This, however, was a vast improvement over the Whitman brace, a rigid, heavy metal arch support that a Boston orthopedist had invented in 1905. It ultimately proved to have little value because it was so uncomfortable, patients couldn't walk in it.

"I think you need orthotics," my mother said while I waited impatiently for my nightly foot massage.

"Why? My feet don't hurt."

"If you wear stilettos, they will."

"But I don't wear stilettos! I wear Stride Rite tie shoes."

"Well, don't blame me . . ."

It was useless to argue, so the following week I had an appointment with the podiatrist. Before I even had a chance to consult with the oracle, he instructed me to take off my shoes and walk up and down the corridor adjacent to the waiting room. My mother had recently told me that I had poor posture and that I should practice walking with a book on my head. She'd read in one of Mrs. Godfrey's magazines that it was standard practice at the John Robert Powers Modeling School. For several weeks, I'd been using Webster's Dictionary, and the top of my head felt sore.

"Could you walk more naturally," the doctor said. "You look like a robot."

I was hoping he'd say "model," and I was mortified. After he watched me walk a few more times, he brought us into the examining room, where he told me to take a seat on the table. He then began to stretch and flex my feet, poking my heels and rotating my ankles.

"Did you ever have any injuries to your feet?" he asked.

"When I was born I did have . . ."

"Jaundice," my mother interjected. "She was the yellowest baby you've ever seen."

"I meant any *foot* problems," he said.

My mother gave me the death stare, so I said, "No problems."

After he finished examining me, we went into his office, which was decorated with framed anatomical drawings of feet. Sitting down at his desk, in front of a foot paperweight, he said, "Your daughter has overpronation."

My mother gasped. "Doctor, is it curable?" She always leapt to the worst conclusions, and in this case, *incurable* meant fewer appointments with him.

He smiled, flashing perfect white teeth. "It's not that serious," he said. The doctor explained that my foot rolled inward more than the ideal, making it difficult for the foot and ankle to stabilize the body.

"Do you do any athletics?" he asked.

During the winter, I went ice-skating with my friend Ginny at the Phillips Academy skating rink. Outsiders called Phillips "Andover" to distinguish it from Phillips Academy in Exeter, but since we lived in Andover, we called it Phillips to distinguish it from the town. For an annual membership fee, nonstudents were allowed to use the rink whenever the Phillips hockey team wasn't practicing.

"I skate at Phillips," I said, hoping the doctor would be impressed with our connections. There was a long waiting list to gain membership.

"Skating is hard when you overpronate," he said.

I was a good skater and suddenly saw my chances of starring in the Ice Capades slipping away.

"Doctor, is there anything you can do about this condition?" my mother asked.

"Your daughter could get orthotics," he said. "I'd be more than happy to fit her. But personally, I'd recommend fencing."

I wasn't sure if I'd heard correctly. *Fencing?* As in Robin Hood? Or *fencing?* As in barbed wire?

He went on to explain that he'd been on the fencing team in college and the sport was excellent for strengthening feet. "It's all about the footwork," he said, getting up from behind his desk to demonstrate a lunge. This was more action than my mother had seen in any of her prior visits, and she was practically swooning. With a pretend sword in hand, he began thrusting and parrying. It was quite a display. As a huge fan of swashbucklers, I immediately pictured myself as a female Errol Flynn. I was beginning to like the podiatrist more and more.

"Would you be the one teaching her?" my mother asked. If he said yes, I knew I'd be suited up in a fencing jacket and knickers in no time.

The podiatrist put down his imaginary sword. "Oh, no," he said. "When would I do it?"

"On weekends?" I offered.

"I'm afraid not."

The doctor said that if we were serious, we could call his office and he'd give us a few names.

Walking home, I told my mother that I hoped we'd be able to find an instructor because I could feel my foot rolling inward and that if I didn't have fencing lessons, I'd probably have to give up skating and wind up in a wheelchair.

"Fencing lessons?" she said. "Your father is going to have *plenty* to say about that."

My father was now head of the mortgage department at the Arlington Trust Company, where most of the people he gave loans to were known either to him or to other people at the bank. If anyone ever defaulted, which they rarely did, his job was on the line. "The best way to gauge a person's ability to pay a mortgage," he'd say, "is by looking them directly in the eye." The bank was located in Lawrence, which had once been a thriving textile center but by the early 1960s was beginning a downward slide that would continue for the next fifty years. The mills were being shuttered, leaving miles of abandoned redbrick buildings and thousands unemployed. Breaking up the dreary skyline was a spectacular clock tower that resembled Big Ben, but the clock had stopped running in the 1950s, a potent reminder that the city's prosperous days were behind it.

The bank was about twenty minutes from our house. Except on Fridays when he worked until nine P.M. and on the nights he had board meetings, my father would arrive promptly at six P.M. for a six fifteen P.M. dinner. It was amazing how much trouble my mother could stir up in such a short time.

"Patricia wants to take fencing lessons," she called to him from the other side of the powder room. "Don't you think it's totally ridiculous? She'll kill herself."

"Supper's ready," my grandfather announced. My sister, Emily, who was then four, was excavating her meat loaf for bones or gristle or other significant fossils. She later toyed with the idea of being an archeologist, so maybe she had a gift for analyzing remains, but we considered her an unusually picky eater.

She was also a genius at inducing my gag reflex at the dinner table. "Stop poking at your meat," my mother said. "Just put it in your mouth."

My sister held up something on her fork. "It's part of a cow's ear," she said.

"I think I'm going to throw up," I said.

"Just take me out feetfirst," my grandfather muttered.

My father bolted down his food so he'd have a chance to read the newspaper before tackling the bills.

"Oh, by the way," my mother said, "the doctor says that Patricia's a pronator. Something about her feet not supporting her body and she may fall over and get a concussion."

I had to admit the concussion bit was a nice touch. I wish I'd thought of it.

"But fencing?" she went on. "It's crazy. Who on earth takes fencing lessons?"

"Lots of people," I said. "Like the guy who plays Zorro."

"Can we talk about it later?" my father pleaded. He'd been home for only fifteen minutes, and one daughter had discovered an ear in her meat loaf and the other had foot problems that hadn't existed when he left for work ten hours earlier.

My father had excellent feet. During the five and a half years he served in the Army during World War II, he was known as one of the few soldiers who "never fell out of a march." I suspect it was more determination than anatomy.

After dinner, I did my homework while Emily watched. Now that she was no longer a baby, we shared a bedroom, and with our nearly seven-year age difference, we weren't ideal roommates. Though Emily was quiet, she loved getting attention and often did it at my expense. When she woke up in the morning, she'd rock back and forth in her bed so that her already squeaky frame squeaked even louder. When she wouldn't stop no matter how many times I'd tell her to "quit it!" I'd call my mother. "Emily's making her bed squeak," I'd say. Of course, Emily by then was "sound asleep," her head resting on her folded hands, looking like a little angel. The minute my mother would leave, the squeaking would begin again. This went on for months without my mother catching Emily, who continued to perfect her timing and angelic pose.

It was hard to focus on my homework with Emily staring at me. "Can't you do something else?" I implored. "Like play with your dolls?"

Bumpa and my mother had finished washing the dishes and he was now rubbing her feet with his "healing hands." I had a sudden brainstorm. What if I offered to trade my foot massage for fencing lessons?

"You are *not* getting fencing lessons," my mother said.

I offered Emily a deal. If she donated her massage time, I'd personally inspect her food and let her stare at me for an entire week. She was so happy that I was paying attention to her that she agreed. A forty-five-minute massage was too good for my mother to pass up, so two weeks later, I was holding a sabre in my hand.

꘎

The podiatrist had recommended a fencing club in Cambridge, not far from Harvard. It was twenty miles away, not exactly convenient, but my mother, sensing my fencing career wouldn't be a long one, agreed to take me to my first lesson. I was told to wear "fencing shoes," but Reinhold's didn't stock them, and the salesman said I had the honor of being the first girl to ever ask for a pair. My mother bought me white Converse sneakers instead. We were loyal to Converse because they manufactured all their canvas products in the old Tyer Rubber plant on Railroad Street. The ugly gray building ran parallel to the train tracks and was on the downhill side of Andover, with Phillips Academy at the top. In 1908, Converse produced the first shoe made exclusively for basketball—the Converse All-Stars. It was later renamed the Chuck Taylor All-Stars, after the Indiana basketball player, and it went on to become the most successful sports shoe in American history.

I never liked going anywhere near the plant because it smelled of burning rubber. It gave me a headache and made me dizzy, and usually I held my nose until we passed it. For a brief time after high school, my mother worked as a secretary there, and even she said the fumes made her ill. She was in a bad mood on the way to Cambridge. She'd given up her weekly appointment with Mrs. Godfrey to take me to fencing and needed her color done because she was pulling out her stilettos that night for a cocktail party. Though she'd once been a natural blonde, she now dyed her hair Frivolous Fawn, a yellowish brown that was perfect for evading shotguns but a little drab outside of hunting season. I wanted her to go platinum like Marilyn Monroe, whose distinctive wiggle was attributed to wearing shoes with two different heel heights. This turned out to be a myth. When Salvatore Ferragamo, Marilyn's shoemaker of choice, hosted a fiftieth anniversary exhibition in honor of her death, the star's stilettos were all the same height. Still, it was Marilyn who helped make the stiletto famous. "I don't know who invented the high heel," she said in her breathy voice, "but all women owe him a lot."

The fencing instructor was waiting for us in a large wood-paneled room, with horizontal lines on the floor and a coil of rope and bladed weapons on the wall. A row of masks lined a long table. It looked like an executioner's chamber and I was beginning to have second thoughts. The instructor, who had bright-blue eyes and curly blond hair, informed us that he was training for the Olympic team. My mother made it clear that competing in the Olympics wasn't my goal and that she'd be happy if I could just walk properly. "She has problems with her feet," she explained. "They don't support her body."

That I was standing upright temporarily confused him, but he recovered enough to ask, "Does she have balance issues? That might be a problem with fencing."

"She doesn't have balance problems—yet," my mother said. "It's just that her feet don't work and fencing is supposed to correct that."

"Who told you that?" he asked.

"My podiatrist," my mother said. "He's also a fencer."

I suspected he'd never received a referral from a fencing podiatrist before, and despite the doctor's directive, he was nervous about working with me. What if I lost my balance and fell on my sword? He'd be disqualified from the Olympics and put on trial for negligent homicide all because I wanted to take fencing lessons. Reluctantly, he walked me down to the far end of the room to show me the three weapons used in competition: the foil, sabre, and épée. "Here's a mask," he said. "You can try it on if you want." It looked like something a beekeeper might wear and smelled of perspiration and something else, something vaguely familiar. He began to explain how the weapons differed and which parts of the body they were allowed to target—the torso, neck, and groin. He gave me a sabre, holding his hand tightly over mine to prevent any accidents. The smelly mask was really getting to me, and I recognized the odor: Tyer Rubber. It was coming from my new Converse sneakers.

"I think I'm a little dizzy," I said.

"Is it your balance issues?" he asked.

"Maybe."

He helped me take off the mask, and putting an arm around my waist, he walked me back to my mother.

"I don't know what kind of podiatrist you're seeing," he said, "but giving a dizzy girl fencing lessons is the craziest thing I've ever heard. The doctor should have his medical license revoked." He patted me on the shoulder and wished me good luck.

"What was that all about?" my mother asked in the car.

I shrugged. "I don't think fencing is for me."

"I didn't think so. You could kill yourself, and then where would you be?"

"Dead, I guess."

"Maybe we should look into orthotics?"

I felt guilty that she'd canceled her appointment with Mrs. Godfrey when she had an affair to attend. I pictured her standing around in her stilettos, trying to make small talk, while Frivolous Fawn died a slow invisible death on top of her head. How bad could orthotics be?

"Yeah," I said, "I think I need them."

"Good, that's settled." She was beaming. "I'll call the foot doctor first thing Monday morning."

4

Wedgies

$\mathcal{M}$ ost cultures have coming-of-age ceremonies that begin when a boy or girl reaches puberty. Young Hamar boys of Ethiopia prove their manhood by running four times over the backs of their cattle, while South American girls of the Tikuna tribe are painted black and made to sing, dance, and jump over fires for several days. While these may strike Westerners as strange, a Tikuna girl transported to America might assume that our coming-of-age ritual involved walking on two sharp objects wrapped in a slaughtered cow.

I recently attended the confirmation of two nieces who live in Greenwich, Connecticut, and also accompanied the younger one to a friend's bat mitzvah. Dozens of young girls spilled out of SUVs wearing what appeared to be their mother's high heels. I spotted a pair of Louboutins. Around the same time, a friend who lives in Manhattan complained that her thirteen-year-old insisted that she "needed" four-inch heels for all the parties she was attending. My friend, who doesn't even own heels, ultimately gave in. In case I didn't believe what the shoes looked like, she sent me a picture. They were extraordinary in their scale and complexity and would have served her daughter well as a pint-size dominatrix, if she hadn't nearly fallen flat on her face as she toppled into the car at the end of the evening.

Even before Suri Cruise set off the dubious trend when she was photographed, at the age of three, in peep-toe silver heels, privileged children in the seventeenth century wore high heels to emulate their parents. Back then, however, there weren't as many designers to pounce on the burgeoning kiddie market, such as Michael Kors, with his three-inch "silver bandage style" espadrilles, and Kenneth Cole, who created a whole line of sophisticated heels, including a Dance Away dress shoe with a "girly glam" bow. My youngest sister, Nancy, who was born when my mother was forty-two, also loves shoes and for Christmas one year, she gave her seven-year-old daughter, Isabel, Christian Louboutin's special edition Barbie Shoe Collection. The shoes came with Louboutin's signature red soles and miniature shoe bags and boxes. "At least Isabel can't fit into them," Nancy said, "and Barbie's feet are already permanently arched so she won't suffer any major foot injuries."

"And she's a doll."

"That too."

An article in *The New York Times*, citing the "Mini-Me" trend, quoted a podiatrist who said that toddlers and preteens, with their softer bones and lack of coordination skills, were more likely to injure their feet and ankles. When the article was posted on Facebook, dozens of mothers decried the fashion, lamenting how young girls were being sexualized. But high heels have always functioned as a symbolic passport to the mysterious adult world of escalating adventures.

When I was confirmed in 1963, the desired shoe was the wedgie, which had a small heel that resembled a Chunky bar, and a squared-off toe. It was the only shoe we were allowed to wear for our debut as adult Christians and, as a result, it achieved icon status far beyond its innocuous style. Though the nuns at St. Augustine's School varied in age and temperament, they were of one mind when it came to fashion. We didn't have uniforms until seventh grade, so we were free to exercise our best judgment as long as our sartorial choices didn't involve excessive flesh or the flaunting of undergarments. As far as our shoes went, we'd been operating under the flats-only rule since kindergarten. If we dared show up in even the most microscopic heel, we'd be labeled a "brazen hussy" and sent to Sister Superior's office.

One of my classmates, Bridget, who lived near Tyer Rubber, was always in trouble for footwear violations. She had numerous older sisters, who passed along their hand-me-downs, including shoes that looked suspiciously like slippers. I couldn't escape Bridget. The nuns lined up everybody according to height, and since we were among the tallest girls, we wound up spending far too much time together. Bridget had a cavity in her front tooth that first appeared in third grade, and I'd watched it grow every year until it assumed the size of a sesame seed. With so many children in the family, I guess it was hard for her parents to keep up with everybody's teeth, especially the loose baby ones. Bridget was the first person to tell me there wasn't a tooth fairy, and when I said I didn't believe it, she called me a stupid dodo. I retaliated by telling her that I'd been born with twelve toes.

"I've seen worse." She shrugged.

For the past six months, we'd all been hearing rumors of "the Talk." Not having older sisters, I asked Bridget to fill me in while we lined up for a fire drill. "It's about the Curse," she said matter-of-factly. Seeing my blank face, she put it more bluntly: "It's about blood. Lots and lots of it." I stared at her tooth, my head spinning. Suddenly, her cavity had turned into the rabbit hole in *Alice in Wonderland,* and I stepped back to avoid tumbling down it.

A few days later, when my mother sat down on the edge of my bed, I was prepared for the worst.

"Patricia, you're twelve now," she began. "In eight months, you'll be . . ."

"What?—*Dead?*"

"No, not dead. Why do you have to be so dramatic about everything? You'll be thirteen. A teenager. Almost a woman. So I think it's time you learned a little something about *meninstration.*" My mother occasionally mangled words, particularly ones she didn't want to pronounce.

"Men! In Stration?" I cried. "Who are these men? Members of the mob?" Was it too late to reconsider fencing?

My mother handed me a pink booklet with a picture of a girl smelling a daisy on the cover. "If you want more information, you can read this, but don't discuss it with anybody. It's personal and private."

After she left, I immediately delved into *The Voyage: Journey of an Egg.* I was desperate to learn how to deal with the "men," but it was all about eggs, *my* eggs, and their bold journey down my fallopian tubes. If one didn't get "fertilized," it was shed along with the lining of my uterus, "thereby producing menstrual discharge."

Blood!

For some odd reason, the girl in the booklet didn't seem to mind having her "friend" visit every month. I figured she must have been awfully hard up for companions. There was a list of "things to avoid," such as "no swimming." It hardly seemed fair that while your eggs were on a voyage, slipping and sliding down your fallopian tubes, you were marooned on land with a bulky napkin strapped between your legs.

Several weeks later, Sister Superior descended from her office to deliver another "talk." She rarely appeared unless it was for something extremely important, such as reminding us that one of Priscilla Lane's movies was going to be on TV, or shaking us down for money to assist the Maryknoll missionaries. We all stood up and delivered the standard greeting: "How are you today, Sister Superior?" to which she'd answer, "Very well, class. Now take your seats." Physically, she wasn't an imposing woman. With her pale skin and clear-framed eyeglasses, she was practically see-through, but despite her short stature and watery face, she was a match for any boy in school. If brutal and aggressive cheek pinching qualified as a martial art, she'd have been a grand master.

After sending the boys to the adjacent cloakroom, where they pretended to hang themselves on the coat hooks, she passed out prayer cards with a picture of Maria Goretti on the front. Maria Goretti was the patron saint of teenage girls, and since we were fast approaching adolescence, Sister Superior wanted to share her story with us. From my experience, these stories were usually pretty gruesome, which is one reason why popes favored red shoes. They evoked the blood of Christian martyrs.

Sister Superior stared at us with her moist yellow eyes. "When Maria was twelve, she attracted the unwanted attention of a male neighbor on the Feast of the Most Precious Blood," she explained. "Maria was in her house, sewing garments for her family. The neighbor tried to strangle her, but Maria fought back. So he held a knife to her throat and cried, "Submit or die!" Maria responded, "Death but not sin!" and he became so angry he stabbed her. Not once, not twice, but a total of fourteen times."

I hoped the story would take a more positive turn, but since people didn't achieve sainthood without dying, I realized it didn't look good for poor Maria.

"Miraculously, she lived for the next twenty hours," Sister Superior said. "During that time, she forgave her murderer. He was so moved by her compassion, he eventually wound up in a monastery, where he worked as a receptionist.

"So what is the moral of this story, girls?" she asked.

All forty of us were completely stumped. Sister Superior waited impatiently until Bridget raised her hand and stood up.

"The moral is you don't have to kill someone to become a receptionist," she said. "One of my sisters has that job and she didn't even graduate from high school."

"*Sit down!* Now, obviously you girls haven't listened to a word I've said. Death but not sin—that's the moral. And as you prepare for your confirmation, I expect you to live by that rule."

⚜

Realizing that I didn't have the right temperament to become a martyr, my mother thought it was important for me to learn ballroom dancing in order to eventually attract a husband. The November Club was *the* place for boys and girls on the cusp of puberty to grasp the essentials of civilized living. These included the waltz, the foxtrot, and "small talk." The November Club had started out in the late 1800s as a women's club, the first in New England to have its own separate building, in this case a dark and spooky Shingle-style house near Phillips Academy. Dancing and etiquette lessons were provided on Tuesday afternoons. Boys had to wear jackets and ties, girls white gloves and their best Sunday dresses and shoes. I chose black patent-leather flats, even though the nuns had told us to avoid shoes with shiny surfaces because they reflected your underpants and boys could see right up your dress. It sounded ridiculous and I didn't buy it, though I hoped I wouldn't find out later that Maria Goretti favored patent leather.

The routine never varied. The boys sat on one side of the room, the girls on the other. At some point, an ancient woman, who was probably in her fifties, made us go through a receiving line so we could introduce ourselves to our volunteer "hosts." As we lined up, boy-girl-boy-girl, I wound up next to the cutest boy in the room. His name was Nathan, and his father taught at Phillips and had done something heroic, like survive multiple torpedo attacks during World War II or climb Mount Everest. Nathan oozed self-confidence and approached the receiving line as if he'd been doing it all his life. "Hello, Mr. and Mrs. Watson," he said. "I'd like to present my friend, Miss Patricia Morrisroe." Holding out my white-gloved hand, I temporarily became tongue-tied and kept staring down at Mrs. Watson's shoes. They were decorated with ladybugs. Finally, I opened my mouth. I'd recently been listening to the cast album of *My Fair Lady*—Julie Andrews was my idol—and in my best Henry Higgins diction, I managed to say, "How kind of *you* to let me come."

"Are you British, dear?" Mrs. Watson asked.

"My grandmother was born in London."

Since we'd just learned that discussing the weather was a great icebreaker, I mentioned that in "Hartford, Hereford, and Hampshire, hurricanes hardly ever happen."

"Oh, how nice," she said. Nathan nudged me along, and we returned to our segregated spots. I tried not to stare at him, but he was adorable, with a long forelock that kept falling over one eye. I hoped he'd ask me to dance, but he made a beeline to a pretty girl with blond hair. I was left sitting on the sidelines with someone who'd broken her leg in a riding accident. She was small and cute, so if she'd been able to walk, I'm sure she'd have been dancing too.

Though it's nice to be tall when you're older, it's a handicap when you're towering above the majority of available partners. For the rest of the semester, I danced with other tall girls, or girls with premature acne, girls with weird hair, girls with thick eyeglasses, fat girls, skinny girls. We took turns leading so we wouldn't alienate the boys even further when and if we ever got a chance to dance with them.

We progressed from the waltz to the foxtrot and then to the rhumba. One afternoon, as a special surprise, we even learned the Mexican hat dance. During the last class of the semester, when I'd all but written off the whole experience, Nathan asked me to dance. I was over the moon. He only came up to my shoulder, but I tried through my untested powers of mental telepathy to convince him that I was cute and petite. After we finished the foxtrot, I thanked him for the dance. As we were all leaving, I saw him huddled together with his friends and I waved good-bye—a bold move for me. Afterward, I heard him say, "What a scarecrow!"

When my mother came to pick me up, I started to cry and told her I hated the November Club and everything it represented.

"What does it represent?" she asked. "The foxtrot? What's so awful about that? We paid good money for you to learn how to dance, and now you're hysterical? Really, Patricia."

When I got home, I exiled my patent-leather flats to the inner reaches of my closet. They were no longer shoes but clumps of hay that could easily be made into a scarecrow whose purpose was to frighten away cute boys with impeccable manners. To this day, I still can't foxtrot, or make small talk, but I do like patent leather.

Richard Cardinal Cushing, who had offered the invocation at President Kennedy's inaugural, was set to preside at our confirmation, and we had spent hours practicing. He was required to give each confirmand a symbolic slap on the cheek as a reminder that we had to be strong in defense of our faith. The Cuban Missile Crisis had happened six months earlier and the nuns were obsessed with Castro. In case he showed up in Andover wearing battle fatigues and chomping on a cigar, we had our instructions. Even if he threatened to pull out our fingernails or tongues, we had to resist committing a sacrilegious act, such as spitting on the crucifix or stomping on Communion wafers. It was a test of our will, and like Maria Goretti, we could respond only one way: "Death—but not sin."

The nuns were even more fearful of Nikita Khrushchev, who had such deplorable manners that in 1960, at the UN General Assembly, he banged his shoe on the table. (His granddaughter, Nina, later explained that he'd taken it off, complaining that it was too tight.) The nuns considered his actions the height of barbarity, and if the Communists took over the country, Khrushchev would outlaw our faith and take away our shoes.

I'd watched President Kennedy's Missile Crisis speech with my mother and the Avon lady. She'd dropped by to deliver my mother's Topaz perfumed cream, which came in a yellow milk-glass jar. Since we were on the brink of nuclear war, my mother was having second thoughts about the body cream and wondered if she could return it. My mother didn't like the Avon lady. She was beautiful and single and wore her platinum hair in a stylish chignon and owned a variety of high heels. She roomed with an elderly couple at the end of our block, and in addition to selling Avon products, she worked at a hospital not far from my father's bank. After she asked him if he could give her a ride in the mornings, my mother thought her pushy and aggressive and wondered what the neighbors would think.

She was giving the Avon lady the cold shoulder when Kennedy came on TV.

He looked grim and puffy-eyed, not the way I remembered him when he was running for president and my mother and I saw him in person. Jackie was there, and it had just rained and the grass was soaking wet. I was pleased to see that she was wearing wedgies, although hers were more sophisticated than anything at Reinhold's. Jackie, who was a size 10, favored low-heeled pumps by Ferragamo or Delman. In a letter to her personal shopper at Bergdorf Goodman, she wrote that she expected her shoes to be "elegant and timeless." As Kennedy spoke, Jackie stood very still, her wedgies sinking lower and lower into the soggy grass. She didn't take her eyes off her husband, even as her shoes were totally getting ruined, and afterward, she didn't even glance down to check on them but continued to smile and shake everyone's hand.

‰

With all the talk of nuclear war and the Communists invading Andover, wedgies were the only bright spot in what was shaping up to be a very tumultuous year. With Nancy's arrival, my parents turned the dining room into a nursery until they cound find a larger house. Not only was sister Emily continuing to find weird things in her food, she now had a weird thing in the dining room, and she wasn't happy about it. At five, she was no longer the baby, but now occupied the unenviable spot of being the middle child.

At some point, my mother asked us to clean up our toys to make room for the baby's paraphernalia. In the process of sorting through our things, my mother told me to put "Betty," my nearly life-size doll, in the attic. Betty had been my companion for years, and while I was at the age when I didn't actually play with her, I didn't necessarily want her in the attic. Before I had a chance to voice my objections, Emily, who'd never shown any prior interest in Betty, decided that she wanted her. In retrospect, I understand what was happening. With a new baby in the house, my middle sister was consolidating her power base. If my mother had a baby, Emily needed a bigger one to equalize things. But as that kind of analysis was beyond me, I refused to yield the doll. We got into a tug-of-war, and in a perfect illustration of family typecasting, I emerged with Betty's head, my sister with the body. With no one getting Betty "whole," my mother sent her to the attic, where she remained, in two separate boxes, until she finally wound up at the dump.

Meanwhile, our dog Buff developed cataracts, a whitish blue seeping through his brown eyes like globs of spilled milk. Even though he couldn't see, he regularly crossed a busy intersection, impregnating several dogs in the neighborhood. This was too much for my mother, who couldn't take care of a baby and a blind dog, especially one whose morals were on par with Maria Goretti's assassin. "That dog's a sex maniac," my mother complained. One of them had to go, and even though Emily voted for Nancy, my mother took the dog to the vet's and we never saw him again.

With only a week to spare before confirmation, we finally made it to Reinhold's.

"You're a little late, aren't you?" the salesman said. "There's been a run on wedgies."

He pulled out the Brannock Device to measure my foot, but given the urgent circumstances, I told him not to bother. "I'm a 7AAA," I said as he disappeared into the back room, while I slumped in one of the metal chairs.

"This is a disaster," I said. "I'm not going to be able to be confirmed without wedgies."

"That's ridiculous," my mother replied. "You think God cares about wedgies?"

The salesman was in the back room for longer than usual, and I was so nervous I was practically hyperventilating. My classmate Mary Kay Phinney, whose father owned the local TV and stereo shop, walked in the door. Though she lacked Hannah Howard's Hollywood pedigree, she was blond and pretty and always had a tan. She needed wedgies too. I looked down at her feet. Luckily, they were smaller than mine.

"There's been a run on wedgies," I announced.

"There's been a run on wedgies!" she yelled to her mother, who was pacifying her two younger children by shoving nickels into the gumball machine.

The salesman finally returned from the back room, carrying one box instead of the usual half a dozen. "I have good news and bad news," he said. "The good news is that I have wedgies. The bad news is that the closest to your size is an 8A."

"I'll take them," I said.

"You better try them on first," my mother advised. "It would be terrible if you had to return them." Even the salesman had to suppress a laugh, given my mother's habit of returning practically every shoe she ever purchased.

I walked over to the fluoroscope and back. They felt pretty good. I figured my feet had probably grown.

"They're perfect," I said.

Afterward, we went across the street to the Dame Shoppe, where women purchased their "intimates" and men rarely ventured, unless it was Valentine's Day and they were stuck for a gift. I'd never bought anything there, but my mother said I needed "hose." I hadn't thought much beyond wedgies, though I had a dim recollection of Sister Superior, after dragging one of the boys by the cheek into the cloakroom, telling us we could wear nylon stockings. I thought nylons were the most useless garments ever invented. My mother would buy a pair and immediately get a run in them. Though she'd try to stop it with clear nail polish, the run would keep running, and then she'd have to throw them in the trash. It was a constant source of frustration. While my father kept his socks for years, my mother, if she was lucky, kept her nylons for a week. There was something terribly unfair about this, but when I mentioned it to my mother, she said it was the price you paid for being a woman.

"Can I help you?" asked one of the saleswomen. She was standing in front of a glass counter containing bras with cups the size of beach balls. I couldn't take my eyes off them, and my mother said it was rude to stare, but I couldn't help it. I could have fit ten of my own breasts inside one cup and still have room for *The Complete Jane Austen*. I spotted Priscilla Lane—Mrs. Howard—walking into the store. My mother was shy so she didn't say hello, but I waved. Mrs. Howard gave me a dazzling movie star smile and a smoky hello. She had a great husky voice that I hoped I'd have one day when I matured, smoked cigarettes, and fulfilled my lifelong dream of becoming an actress.

"We'd like a pair of nylons," my mother said as Mrs. Howard perused a rack of lacy nightgowns. The saleswoman showed us several color samples ranging from nude to tangerine. We settled on nude, and then the woman pulled out a plastic box containing garter belts. "Do you want something plain or fancy?" she asked. I wanted neither. Though we'd learned about Newton's law of gravity in science class, it hadn't dawned on me that nylons wouldn't stay up on their own. I selected a plain blue garter belt and just wanted to get out of there, but the saleswoman, staring at my chest, suggested to my mother that I needed a training bra. "You wouldn't want them to jiggle," she whispered, bending over the counter to reveal her bottomless cleavage.

My breasts didn't jiggle. They barely existed. And what did breasts need to be "trained" for? A sword fight with a baby?

The saleswoman handed me something that looked like a white wraparound bandage and told me to go into the dressing room and try it on. On one side was Mrs. Howard, on the other a woman being fitted for a nursing bra. *Milk spillage?* Did the saleswoman actually say, *"Milk spillage"*? My mother never nursed any of us, and I didn't know any other mothers who'd dream of letting their children anywhere near their breasts. Hadn't this woman ever heard of baby formula? You mixed it up, poured it into a bottle, and stuck it in the baby's mouth, thereby doing away with bizarre problems like milk spillage. I was getting ill. Even my new wedgies didn't compensate for the newfound horrors of becoming a woman.

"How ya' doin' in there, hon?" the saleswoman asked.

"I need more time," I said, thinking in terms of decades.

I reluctantly took off my white Lollipop undershirt with its delightful pink rosebud and pulled the bra over my head. The saleswoman, overstepping all civilized notions of privacy, barged in and began fiddling with the bra. "There!" she said. "Now that really holds you in." Bind was more like it. The bra flattened me so completely I could have been playing Viola disguised as Cesario in *Twelfth Night*.

Mrs. Howard and I emerged from the dressing room at the same time. She had something black and slinky in her arms. I stepped on her foot and in the midst of apologizing dropped my training bra.

She picked it up for me. "Oh, thanks," I said casually, as if shopping for brassieres was something I did all the time.

"I'll *die* before wearing this thing," I whispered to my mother, who was debating whether she needed a new girdle to get herself back into pre-Nancy shape.

"You could use a girdle too," she said.

I was a gawky five feet eight and weighed 110 pounds. Nothing jiggled, nothing wiggled, nothing moved at all.

"I don't want a girdle," I said. "I don't want a bra. I don't even want these stupid nylons or this garter belt." My mother gave me the death stare. I was causing a scene. In a store. With a movie star nearby.

"Why do you have to make such a big deal out of everything?" my mother whispered loud enough for the saleswoman to overhear.

"You're just overwhelmed, hon," the saleswoman said. "It's like when I had my first baby and I was screaming, 'Just knock me out, because this kid is ripping me apart.'"

Yeah, just like that.

⁂

On confirmation day, I couldn't attach the nylons to the garters, and my mother said, "You'd better learn because they're now a part of you." She wasn't kidding. Within minutes, they'd left figure-eight marks on my thighs. With the slippery hose, my wedgies were now too big and I could barely keep them on.

With his Kodak Instamatic in hand, Daddy asked me to go outside so he could take a picture to commemorate the day. I followed him out to the front lawn, where he usually took all our pictures, posing us next to the cherry blossom trees, which depending on the season and Daddy's eye were either gloriously in bloom or not in the photo at all. Since he didn't like to impose himself on people, he never set up his shots properly, and if somebody was blinking or grimacing or looking away, he still snapped the picture. Photography was too intimate an activity for him and he could do it only by doing it quickly. And yet, away from us, removed from direct personal contact, he'd spend hours pasting the photographs into albums, writing, in his perfect script, little notes, such as *Patricia celebrates her First Communion* or *Patricia on her sixth birthday*. He'd date everything, every single picture, so we'd have a record, a history, and I loved looking at the albums. They were among my favorite items in the house.

"Okay," Daddy said, "why don't you stand in front of the cherry blossoms?"

I straightened my regulation red skullcap, smoothed my hair, and squinted into the direct sunlight. Daddy took the picture so fast I wondered if he even caught a glimpse of me through the viewfinder. "I think it's going to be a good one," he said. He always said that after taking a photograph. *I think it's going to be a good one.*

Meanwhile, my mother ran around the house doing whatever she did to make us late, while we all sat in the car. Bumpa rolled his eyes, and my father held his breath. I kept waiting for him to exhale, but his face kept getting redder and redder and I thought he'd explode right in the driver's seat, on my confirmation day. Finally, my mother came out and my father literally breathed a sigh of relief. She patted her heart, as if her habitual tardiness were killing her instead of us.

Nancy and Emily were crying. Nancy was upset because Emily had pinched her, and Emily was upset because my mother had yelled at her, and I was upset because my wedgies were too big and I hated my confirmation name—Frances. With all the focus on shoes, I hadn't paid much attention to selecting a middle name. It was supposed to honor a saint, one whose virtues we could emulate. Because

I wanted to live beyond the age of twelve, Maria was out. I finally opted for Frances because I had a crush on a boy named Francis, whose last name I can't remember. He wasn't even that cute and was constantly getting into trouble for making wisecracks. In second grade, Sister Margaret threw him in a trash can and put the lid on it and he stayed in there for several hours without making a sound. Perhaps it was then I developed my crush, or several years later, when he defended a boy who had the weird habit of collapsing on the floor every time he had to diagram a sentence at the blackboard. Clearly, the boy had psychological issues, but since *psychology* wasn't in the nuns' vocabulary, they hit him with a ruler instead. Once when he wouldn't get up, Francis carried him back to his desk and offered him water from his thermos. Afterward, the nun dumped Francis in the trash again, so I suppose he did exhibit saintly qualities in the face of persecution. Still, I wished I'd chosen Hayley.

My mother took out her compact and powdered her nose, which she claimed I disfigured when I accidentally kicked it with my foot. It happened when I was a baby, so it wasn't premeditated or deliberate, but my mother talked about the assault as if I'd been plotting it from conception. "See, one nostril is crooked," she said. "It was never like that."

Both of her nostrils looked fine. They weren't things of great beauty, but whose were?

At church, we formed a processional behind the cardinal, who wore a mitered hat and carried a crook-shaped crosier. Some of the other girls hadn't taken nylons into consideration when buying their wedgies, and we slipped and slid all the way down the aisle. At one point, I stepped out of my shoe and Bridget nearly fell into me, and Francis What's-His-Name laughed.

The cardinal, who had already attended several confirmations that day and was due to preside over several more, quickly got down to business. In a sharp nasal voice, he told us that the word *confirmation* meant a "strengthening" and just as everyone born into the world reached physical maturity, everyone born to the spiritual life through baptism reached spiritual maturity. We had to be ready, with both our bodies and souls, to uphold the true religion. With our sponsors in tow—I'd selected Bumpa—we headed up to the altar to become "soldiers of Christ." Kneeling down at the railing, I steeled myself for "the slap," but the cardinal merely tapped my cheek and then anointed my forehead with oil. As I returned to my seat, I waited for a sign that I'd reached maturity, but the only visible evidence was the run in my nylon stocking galloping at full speed up my leg.

5

Beatle Boots

A few months ago, I was having lunch with my friend Jennifer at the original P. J. Clarke's, where the restaurant's deceased mascot—Skippy the dog—is now a piece of taxidermy above the handicapped bathroom. Jennifer, who has great taste, casually mentioned that she'd recently bought a new pair of boots at a store called R. M. Williams. We were sitting at the discreet table Jackie Onassis was said to prefer, and I'd ordered an organic turkey burger. Since I'm mostly a vegetarian, I felt guilty, as if I'd just gobbled down a Big Mac, or Skippy. After a strong cup of American coffee, I sprinted from P.J.'s to R.M.'s. Normally, a longhorn steer insignia would have put me off, but now that I was a carnivore, I eagerly walked inside. To my delight and utter surprise, I found Beatle boots.

While the Beatles aren't generally associated with the Australian outback, their boots were a modification of Victorian paddock, or jodhpur, boots. These were designed with elastic siding to make them easier to remove. In the 1950s and '60s, when King's Road became a hub for creative artists known as the Chelsea set, fashion designers and models adopted the paddock boot, which was renamed the Chelsea boot. The Beatles, collaborating with the bespoke footwear company Annello & Davide, added a Cuban heel, and the Beatle boot was born.

Paul was my mother's favorite Beatle, which really annoyed me because he was my "fave" too. Parents were supposed to hate the Beatles, not love their music and moon over their photographs. "Don't you think their hair is too long?" I'd say, hoping she'd agree with the majority of older Americans and criticize them for looking like girls. But she thought they were adorable, the kind of boys you'd take home to mother, especially if the mother had a huge crush on one of them. I warned her that Paul's choirboy looks were deceiving, but she claimed I was being "uptight." Suddenly I was the conservative one, criticizing Paul for smoking too much and having a "dark side." "He's worse than Elvis," I said. "At least *he* fought for his country and made inspirational movies like *G.I. Blues*."

My mother hated Elvis. She didn't like Frank Sinatra, either, and she'd been too young to appreciate the first pop sensation—the 1920s megaphone crooner, Rudy Vallee. But now, at forty-four, with three kids, including a two-year-old, she was in the throes of Beatlemania. "Do you think Paul is going to marry Jane Asher?" she'd ask, and I'd have to remind her that she was far too old for him. She'd remind me that while I was closer to his age, I had the disadvantage of being only thirteen and that unless I moved to a country that looked favorably upon child brides, I wouldn't be walking down the aisle anytime soon. Things got so competitive that at one point I told my father that she was in love with someone else. He was reading *The Boston Globe*, so I had to repeat it three times.

"She's leaving to go to Macartneys?" he asked. Macartneys was a clothing store near Reinhold's.

"No, she's leaving you for Paul McCartney. Of the Beatles."

He nodded his head and returned to the paper.

My mother's love affair with Paul did have some advantages. I never had to beg for Beatles albums. She bought them for me the minute they were released, along with all the special-edition fan magazines, as well as *16* and *Tiger Beat*. She knew that Pete Best had been the original drummer and that George was dating Pattie Boyd and that Ringo, whom she insisted on calling the Ugly One, had suffered pleurisy as a child. "They should have kept Pete," she'd say. "At least he was cute."

I had my own record player, a red one that you could snap shut and carry like a suitcase, and sometimes my mother and I would listen to *Meet the Beatles!* while sprawled across my canopy bed. Inevitably, she'd spoil the mood by pointing out my sloppy hospital corners or the pile of dirty clothes on the floor, and I'd threaten to pack up my record player and hit the road. She'd say, "You're lucky to have a mother, unlike Paul, who lost his own mother in 1956, when he was only fourteen." And I'd say, "Yeah, but I bet you don't know how old she was when she died." And she'd say, "Ha! She was forty-seven, and her name was Mary. Anything else you'd like to know?"

Bridget couldn't believe my mother was a Beatles fan. "My mom puts her fingers in her ears every time they come on the radio," she said as we were waiting outside during a practice nuclear bomb evacuation. I warned her to lower her voice because our eighth-grade teacher, Sister Mary Ethelburger, was coming our way. She had heavily lidded eyes, a sloped neck, and thick, curved fingernails; she crept across the school yard on her short, stout legs, rocking from side

to side. Since she taught geography and spoke endlessly of her fasci-
nation with the Galápagos Islands, we thought of her as an ancient
tortoise that had over the centuries migrated to Massachusetts.

No one could decipher her foreign accent. Francis What's-His-
Name came up with the brilliant idea that she was a Russian Jew.
"How many Catholics do you know with the name Burger?" he
asked. It didn't take long for Sister Ethelburger to go from being the
world's biggest land tortoise to assuming the identity of Ethel Rosenberg, the famous spy. We didn't realize that the real Ethel Rosenberg
had been dead for ten years, only that she'd given atomic secrets to the
Russians. In our version, Ethelburger or Ethel *Berger*, had divorced
Mr. Rosenberg, converted to Catholicism, and entered a convent,
where her superior knowledge of nuclear weapons and endangered
species had led to an assignment at St. Augustine's. When the Russians invaded, they'd get the shock of their lives when an elderly nun
threatened to drop the A-bomb or a gigantic tortoise on their heads.

In between learning about the weather conditions on the Galápagos, my friends and I conspired to move to London, where we'd
get jobs as models or at Biba, the famous fashion boutique. Ever since
kindergarten, I'd had the same close friends—Mary, Agnes, and
Susan. Agnes and Susan were best friends, while I was Agnes's
runner-up. Not only was Agnes the smartest girl in class but also the
one most likely to leave Andover for Greenwich Village and have
love affairs with famous artists or heroin addicts. With her long
brown hair and olive skin, she looked like Joan Baez and was always
quoting Bob Dylan. One of her most enviable attributes, especially
at a school that valued handwriting over actual writing, was her
beautiful penmanship. Before one of the nuns confiscated it, she
wrote with a cigarette-shaped pen that she occasionally "smoked,"

driving the boys wild. She had no interest in her peers, however, setting her sights on older, more accomplished men, such as Dylan, or John Lennon, or the Central Catholic High School junior, who wore Jade East cologne. It had Oriental letters on the box and a strange musk smell that Agnes said was a powerful aphrodisiac.

Every spring, the Girl Scouts put on a show to entertain the Brownies, and Agnes thought it would be fun if we impersonated the Beatles. Since John was Agnes's favorite, she wanted to be him, while Susan claimed George, and Mary, who had brown eyes and was left-handed, seemed the logical choice for Paul. That left me with Ringo, who was nobody's favorite, except maybe his mother's, but if she was anything like mine, she probably liked Paul best.

Informed of the news, my mother reacted as if I'd had a sex-change operation and had actually become Ringo. "So you're the Ugly One?" she said. "You're the incredible sad sack with the big nose?"

"Yeah, I guess."

"You should quit the band," she advised. "They clearly don't appreciate you."

Yoko Ono hadn't even appeared on the scene and my mother was all ready to break up the Beatles before we'd made our first appearance. "Ringo," she repeated, shaking her head. "You'd better be careful not to sit on any damp stoops or you could get pleurisy."

For the next two weeks, we practiced lip-synching to "She Loves You," shaking our heads in unison as we mimed the falsetto *ooooohs*. I played percussion with two pencils, while the others played air guitar. It soon became evident that Mary was the breakout star. Her resemblance to Paul was uncanny. She must have practiced his mannerisms for hours, perfecting the way he cocked his head and jutted out his chin, casting his angelic eyes heavenward. When my mother caught us practicing in our basement, she nearly fainted. "It's remarkable," she said. "It's Paul. It's really Paul."

Bumpa made me a cardboard drum set, painting *The Beatles* on the front. I was dying to get a pair of Beatle boots, which I hoped would compensate for the psychological damage that would ultimately result from being Ringo.

"Beatle boots—are you crazy?" was my mother's first reaction. Her second was "Your father is going to have *plenty* to say about that!" Eventually, I wore her down, and we went off to Reinhold's.

"What kind of girl wants Beatle boots?" the salesman asked.

"Girls who impersonate Ringo," my mother said. "He's the Ugly One."

"They're all ugly," he said. "That hair! It's a disgrace."

"Particularly Ringo's," she said.

Fed up with the way they were dumping on my alter ego, I blurted out that my mother was in love with Paul. Her face turned bright red. Realizing that I might have jeopardized my Beatle boots, I added, "You know, of Peter, Paul and Mary." The salesman started singing "Puff the Magic Dragon," encouraging my mother to join in. She only knew that Puff lived by the sea and nothing about Jackie Paper or the land called Hana Lee. For a major Peter, Paul and Mary fan, it was a pretty weak showing, and the salesman looked suspicious.

I reminded him that we'd come for Beatle boots, and he told me they didn't make them for ladies but that he'd try to find a men's pair. "This is getting worse by the minute," my mother whispered. "Now you're going to be wearing men's shoes. Your father is so upset he can hardly speak."

"He doesn't anyway."

The salesman had no concept of Beatles footwear, presenting me with several pairs of construction boots. Since we were years away from the Village People, I showed him a picture I'd torn out from a Beatles magazine. The salesman put on his glasses to study it. "These are like flamenco boots," he said. "You know, *Olé!*" After he disappeared into the stockroom, I asked my mother for some change so I could get a ring from the vending machine. I already had seven, but Ringo wore four on each hand, so I was short one. You never knew what was going to slide down the chute, and I got a plastic tarantula, a devil, and a Rat Fink before scoring big with a skull ring.

"You may be in luck," the salesman said. Opening the first box, he pulled out a black boot with elastic inserts, a side zipper, and a two-inch Cuban heel. After referencing my *Beatles* magazine, I said, "That's it!" The boots even fit.

On the day of the performance, we wore white dickeys, navy blazers, and black slacks, tucking our hair inside our collars to make it look shorter. I was the only one with Beatle boots. Agnes said that since I was behind a fake drum set, nobody would see my feet, but I told her it was important to get into character. The Brownies were in the school auditorium, waiting for the show to begin, while we stood backstage with one of our classmates, who was preparing to do her famous Scottish sword dance. Ellie was dressed in the traditional costume of tartan skirt, white frilly blouse, velvet tam, and lace-up shoes known as ghillies.

There are some people who shouldn't be around swords, and Ellie was one of them. Though agile and light on her feet, she suffered from stage fright and reached levels of near hysteria whenever she had to perform. Her mother was usually on hand to calm her down. "You can do it, you can do it," she kept whispering as her daughter stood shaking in a corner. Because we'd seen her do it a dozen times, we wished she'd dispense with the theatrics and just get on with it. The Brownies were getting restless. Finally, hoisting the two giant swords over her shoulders, she strode onstage and one of the Brownies, thinking she was about to be slaughtered, ran for the exit.

Ellie placed the swords in a cross formation while her mother played recorded bagpipe music. With her arms flung high, she began dancing counterclockwise around the swords before stepping inside them. The goal was not to touch the blades or inflict self-injury. From backstage, we heard the sounds of metal grating against metal. She kept tripping, and I pictured the girl in *The Red Shoes* with her feet all bloodied, or worse, with no feet. Ellie limped off the stage, telling her mother that she needed to go to the emergency room.

After the Brownie leader announced that we'd be taking a short break, the rumor spread that the Scottish dancer was dead. "This is a disaster," Agnes said. "The Brownies are crying."

After the swords were removed, I set up my cardboard drum set and sat on a folding metal chair, while the other girls stood in front of me. As the Brownie leader pulled open the curtain, she cried, "Ladies and gentlemen, the Beatles!" When the Brownies realized we weren't the real thing, they went back to sniffling and comparing merit badges. One fiddled with an Etch A Sketch. The school janitor was in charge of our music, and after we gave him a sign, he placed the needle on the 45 of "She Loves You." When one of the Brownies noticed Mary's startling resemblance to Paul, she let out a scream, setting off a chain reaction. Shaking her head during the *ooooh* part, Mary caused such a sensation that the Brownie with the Etch A Sketch rushed the stage and had to be restrained.

After the performance, the Brownies crowded around Mary, referring to her as Mr. McCartney and asking for her autograph. Things grew so unruly that the Brownie leader suggested we leave the building, and as we ran out, we could hear the girls chanting, "Paul, Paul, Paul . . ."

⚘

Due to our legendary Brownies appearance, we were deluged with offers to perform at kids' birthday parties, so we officially became the Beatle Girls. Mary immersed herself completely in the role, carrying a picture of Jane Asher in her wallet and talking in a Liverpool-by-way-of-Boston accent. No one dared criticize, though, because she was the big draw, the fabbest of the Fab Four.

We bought silver ID bracelets with our designated Beatles name on it, although I cheated and had mine engraved PAUL. On weekends, we strolled around town in our Beatles outfits, hoping to attract attention. Though I was tired of being the Ugly One, I loved my Beatle boots, which despite their two-inch Cuban heels were comfortable even when running away from our fans. One Saturday, we caused a near riot in the frozen food section of the Andover Co-Op. The Brownie with the Etch A Sketch screamed, *"Look! It's the Beatle Girls!"* and Brownies came out of nowhere, chasing us out of the supermarket and down Main Street. It was straight out of *A Hard Day's Night* and we were totally exhilarated, although we feigned annoyance because we were losing our privacy and soon we wouldn't be able to go anywhere without getting mobbed. *"We need to tyke a 'olidye wiff our birds,"* Mary said. *"Some place pryvit, like the Galápagos."*

There was some discussion about getting Beatles haircuts, but none of us wanted to go that far. When I mentioned it to my mother, she didn't think it was such a bad idea. "After all, you have the boots. Why not the hair?" My mother never liked my hair; it was now medium length and naturally straight, which in her mind meant lacking body.

For years she'd been getting perms from Mrs. Godfrey and anything that wasn't tight and curly read "limp." "Why not go to Mrs. Godfrey's and let her take a look," she suggested.

Many of the top British models were wearing their hair in a Vidal Sassoon bob, and I thought it might look cute on me. Armed with a stack of fashion magazines, I told Mrs. Godfrey exactly what I wanted: "Something mod and totally fab." She glanced at the pictures, assuring me that she could easily do any of the styles. Something told me it was a big mistake to let Mrs. Godfrey go anywhere near my head, but since fame had already gone to my head, I wasn't thinking clearly. She began chopping and chopping, and when she was finished, I didn't look like a British model. I didn't look fab. I looked like Moe of the Three Stooges. Not wanting to offend Mrs. Godfrey, who was a perfectly nice woman even if she wasn't Vidal Sassoon, I pronounced it "different."

"It's certainly 'mod,'" she said.

To my mother's eyes, it was worse than mod. It was the dreaded word: *limp.*

"Are you thinking of a perm?" Mrs. Godfrey asked.

My mother nodded.

Two hours later, I arrived home with short curly hair, which, had it been longer, would have counted as Andover's first Afro. "Why is your hair all frizzy?" Bumpa wanted to know. I stared at my mother. "Blame her," I said. It went through my mind that she did it on purpose to get Paul all to herself. When she came upstairs to ask if I wanted to listen to *A Hard Day's Night,* I told her to leave.

"What happened to you?" Agnes said when I walked into the school yard the next morning. "Did you get electrocuted or something?" All Mary could say was "*Blimey!*"

During English, Sister Superior charged into the classroom with some "very disturbing news." We figured the gig was up for Ethel Berger and that she'd be carted away to prison for being a Russian spy and a terrible geography teacher. "I would like to see the Beatle Girls," she said. Thinking she wanted to book us for a performance, Agnes reached for her calendar, but Sister Superior began tapping her wooden clicker against her palm. One by one, we slowly stood up.

"Where's the other Beatle Girl?" Sister Superior asked.

"I think they're all accounted for," Ethel Berger said.

"But aren't there five Beatles?"

"No, you're thinking of the Dave Clark Five," Bridget offered. "Or maybe you think Pete Best's still in the band, but he's not."

"Enough!" Sister Superior said. "Now what in the name of all the saints and angels in heaven do you think you're doing impersonating those hoodlums?"

"The Beatles aren't hoods," Bridget said. "They're rockers who went mod."

"Go to my office, Bridget. I'll deal with you later."

"You four are a total disgrace to womanhood." Sister Superior stared at me. "And *you*? I suppose this is the latest Beatle hairdo?"

"Not really."

"You don't even look like a girl anymore. Boys, would you marry someone with hair like this?"

The boys, deliberating for all of a second, held their noses and screamed, *"Pee-Yew!"* Francis What's-His-Name screamed the loudest, and from then on, I never used my middle name, not even the first initial.

"This charade has gone on long enough," Sister Superior said. "I am officially disbanding the Beatle Girls. Tomorrow, I want you to bring in your Beatles costumes and whatever else you have, and they will be confiscated." Afterward, she made the rounds of all the younger grades, informing them that the Beatle Girls were dead. I'd heard that some of the Brownies cried, but they quickly got over it. The next day, I handed over my plastic rings, my white dickey, and my Beatle boots. I'd left my Paul ID bracelet at home, but Sister Superior didn't seem to notice.

"That's 'orrible about your boots, mate," said Mary, who was still clinging to the last vestiges of fame.

Word must have gotten around, because my mother seemed to know all the details when I got home. My grandfather was waiting for me with my usual snack of a Hostess Yodel and milk.

"I hear the Beatles have been disbanded," she said. "What was the offense?"

"You're looking at it," I said, pointing to my hair.

"That's nonsense, Patricia. It had nothing to do with your hair. I heard Sister Superior took away all your things, including your boots. They cost good money, you know. That's the last time you are ever going to talk me into getting you a pair of stupid shoes."

Now my Beatle boots were stupid. She'd loved the Beatles. Had Sister Superior gotten to her too? While my mother's infatuation with Paul had been annoying, it had elevated her briefly into the realm of extraordinary, and now she was just a plain, unimaginative housewife. "I don't want my Yodel," I said, stomping upstairs.

We didn't speak for the next three days, and then one afternoon, I found my Beatle boots in my closet. "I told Sister Superior you needed them because of your foot problems," my mother explained.

That night, I took off my Paul ID bracelet and placed it on her pillow. It was the least I could do for a fellow Beatles fan.

6

A Ghillie Out of Water

St. Augustine's ended at eighth grade, and instead of following my friends to neighboring Catholic schools, I enrolled at Andover Junior High. It was a huge gamble. The nuns had brainwashed us into thinking the public school kids were practically devil worshippers, and we were advised to avoid them in case we caught their "spiritual disease." The only public school kid I knew was my epileptic neighbor, whose brother rode a Harley with the Hell's Angels, so I feared the worst.

To bolster my self-confidence, I immersed myself in fashion magazines, which Bumpa bought for me out of his small Brooks School pension, warning me to keep it a secret from my mother. With the advent of the Swinging Sixties and its emphasis on youth, high heels were out and Courrèges-style go-go boots and girlish flats were in. Soon, Twiggy would replace Jean Shrimpton as the model everyone wanted to look like and even mature women aspired to her waifish appearance.

It was either in *Mademoiselle* or *Seventeen* that I spotted the perfect "back-to-school" outfit: a corduroy dress with a rounded collar
and Empire waist, textured stockings, and lace-up ghillies. These
were similar to my old schoolmate's sword-dancing shoes. Who
knew she was such a trendsetter? The salesman at Reinhold's had
never heard of ghillies, advising me to stick with Bass Weejuns.
"That's what the girls at the junior high are wearing," he said smugly.
"You'll see . . ."

Most people thought that Weejuns were named after an Indian
tribe, probably because the name sounded like the pejorative *Injun*.
In fact, the word was a slang term for Norwegian fishermen, whose
locally crafted moccasins were "discovered" in the late nineteenth
century when British anglers went salmon fishing in the fjords. By the
1930s, wealthy Americans and Europeans were traveling to Norway,
and after the slippers were spotted in Palm Beach, *Esquire* magazine,
along with Rogers Peet, the men's clothing company, collaborated
with Bass to make a sturdier version. It ultimately became the penny
loafer, and an Ivy League staple.

჻

Right before school started, I convinced my mother to take me to the
Northshore Shopping Center, one of the first and largest malls in
New England. In addition to dozens of stores, it also had a bowling
alley, a twin cinema, a kiddie amusement park, and Mt. Carmel
Chapel, the first religious sanctuary ever to grace a shopping complex. The mall was in Peabody, so "going to Peabody" became synon-
ymous with shopping. En route, we passed the town of Danvers,
which since the late nineteenth century had been home to the state
mental hospital, previously known as the Danvers Lunatic Asylum.
Just as *Peabody* was code for going shopping, *Danvers* was code for

going crazy. As if having a mental institution in the town wasn't creepy enough, Danvers, in its earliest incarnation as Salem Village, had hosted the witchcraft trials. Women were banned from wearing high heels, which were considered the work of the devil.

Nancy, who was three at the time, was sitting on Bumpa's lap in the backseat. Except for our mutual antagonism toward our mother, we had little in common. Nancy's grooming habits were abominable. Having been exposed to Mrs. Godfrey in utero, she'd learned at a very early age never to let anyone near her head. If my mother attempted to untangle one of the many knots dotting her stringy hair, she'd scream so loudly my mother feared the neighbors would call the police. My mother spent so much time worrying about the neighbors, we could have been back in old Salem. In my mother's defense, Nancy's hair did give the appearance of demonic possession, but you had to admire her for not buckling to social convention.

Once we parked the car in the huge lot, Bumpa went off to buy S. S. Pierce orange marmalade, which he spread on his English muffin each morning. I headed to the shoe department at Jordan Marsh, pretending that the woman and ratty-haired kid were taking a break from the mental hospital's production of *Oliver.*

"Oh, this is too much," my mother said as Nancy grabbed a pair of high heels and took off with them. "We're all going to wind up in jail."

While my mother chased Nancy, I found a salesman and asked if they stocked ghillies. I had my magazine ready in case he gave me a blank stare, but he asked, "What color?" I hadn't anticipated having a choice, so I was temporarily overwhelmed.

"I'll bring them all out so you can see *everything*," he said. I'd never knowingly met a homosexual. I didn't even know what the word meant, but he wasn't like any of the boring Reinhold's salesmen, whose sartorial choices leaned toward wrinkled shirts and brown pants. He was wearing a suit, with a colorful pocket square, and a gold pinkie ring. His thick black eyebrows were quite stunning, right down to the pronounced arch. When Nancy returned from her wild shoplifting spree, my mother having returned the heels to their proper place, I was in the process of deciding between taupe or dark brown suede. "Of course brown is more practical," the salesman was saying, "but taupe is *très chic*."

"I'm afraid taupe is going to get too dirty," my mother said, trying not to stare at his brows. "She has foot problems, so she's very hard on her shoes. I think we should go with brown."

"Big mistake!" he said. "Brown is common, and clearly your daughter is not."

I loved the man! Who cared that his brows looked like Elizabeth Taylor's?

"But taupe gets dirty," my mother said weakly.

"Taupe," he pronounced, "is *divine!*"

Except on the late-night movies, my mother had never heard *divine* uttered with such theatrical finesse and authority. There was no arguing with him. The shoes were mine.

Since they were more expensive than my mother had anticipated, she reluctantly put them on her Jordan's charge. It was supposed to be used only in the case of a "dire emergency," although what kind of situation would be so calamitous that you'd need a department store charge was something I never figured out. But that wasn't my business. The important thing was that my father hated credit cards. He hated them more than turnips, which was the only food he disliked. My father paid his bills the day they arrived and didn't believe in racking up debt. My mother's view of finance was a little fuzzier. Every Monday, my father "deposited" her allowance in the "Sock

Trust Company," which was located in his top bureau drawer. She didn't have to deal with checks. All she had to do was unfold a pair of freshly laundered socks, and like magic, the money appeared.

We met up with my grandfather at the Mt. Carmel Chapel, where he was deep in prayer. He was a very religious man and a soft touch for charity. He'd recently "adopted" a girl from South Africa through a Catholic relief organization. Every month, he sent money to the girl's family, and Mosa sent letters and pictures back. She wanted to go to school in the United States, and my mother was afraid she'd show up at our doorstep one day. There was only one African American family in Andover. They'd lived in the town for several generations, but we never saw them. "I'm not sure how she'll fit in," my mother said, looking at a blurry picture of Mosa standing next to a goat.

While my grandfather finished up his prayers, Nancy managed to get into the box of blueberry muffins he'd picked up at Jordan's bakery. The muffins had gigantic tops coated with at least a half cup of sugar, and the blueberries were hot and gooey. "You can't eat muffins in church," my mother whispered, yanking her outside. Nancy didn't like to be pulled any more than she liked getting her hair brushed. Assuming a defensive crouch, she flopped on the floor of the Catholic bookstore and wouldn't get up until my mother bribed her with a St. Christopher key ring.

"Did you get the shoes?" my grandfather asked as we walked to the car.

"She thinks money grows on trees," my mother said.

"No, I don't. It grows in socks."

"Shhhh!" she whispered, as if we were discussing a money-laundering scheme instead of one that involved actual laundry. "All I can say is that you better live and die in those ghillies."

I died in them. I died a thousand deaths and that was only the first day of school. The salesman at Reinhold's had been right. The girls at the junior high weren't wearing ghillies. They weren't wearing mod dresses or textured tights. They were wearing Bass Weejuns, along with cable cardigans and floral print dresses and A-line skirts. The most popular brand was The Villager, the brainchild of Max Raab, a Jewish Philadelphian who was known as the Dean of the Prep Look. A man of widely divergent interests, he not only popularized the conventional WASP style, but he also optioned Anthony Burgess's *A Clockwork Orange*, about futuristic gang violence in England. He'd wanted the Beatles to star in it, but when that didn't work out for reasons obvious to any Beatles fan, he hooked up with the director Stanley Kubrick and served as the film's executive producer.

The girl opposite me kept staring at my shoes in a way that made me feel even more self-conscious. She was wearing a blue dress decorated with pink ladybugs and Weejuns. Her long dark hair had a low side-part, and she'd tucked a portion of it behind her ears. I glanced around the classroom. Half the girls had the exact same hairstyle with the exact same side-part. Though my perm had grown out, my hair was still very short. Mrs. Godfrey had given me a pair of fake pearls for eighth-grade graduation, and I was so touched I sacrificed myself to her scissors. To call the result Twiggy-esque would have given the erroneous impression that I actually had hair.

"I think I need Weejuns," I said when I came home after school.

My mother looked as if her head was about to spiral off her neck and go into orbit. "Weejuns?" she shouted. "Are you crazy? We just bought you those ghillies. What do you expect us to do with them?"

"Maybe we can send them to Mosa," suggested Bumpa, who was grinding lamb for shepherd's pie, while Emily monitored for eyeballs.

"Dad, they're taupe!" my mother said.

"What's wrong with that?"

"Mosa lives in a mud hut! They'll be filthy in two seconds."

At that moment, my piano teacher, Miss Wilhelmina Hagenauer, arrived at the door. She'd also been my mother's piano teacher and still only charged only $2 a lesson, including gas. Miss Hagenauer was in her mid-seventies and, as my grandfather put it, "bigger than a grand piano." In addition, she suffered from narcolepsy, and at the beginning of every lesson, she'd always ask for a pot of very strong tea and then spend the next hour dozing. By the time she taught Nancy, she didn't even bother with the tea and went straight to sleep. As a result, none of us ever learned to read music, but for some mysterious reason, we all played extremely well. Miss Hagenauer hoped I'd go to the New England Conservatory of Music, where if nothing else I'd finally learn the difference between a half and quarter note.

After my lesson, my mother paid Miss Hagenauer, who tucked the money into a paisley case that contained an embroidered hankie and two automatic pencils. As she was getting ready to leave, she asked how I liked my new school. "She hates the ghillies," my mother said. Miss Hagenauer, who was slightly disoriented from sleeping through my rousing performance of Chopin's Polonaise Militaire, thought *ghillies* was slang for *girls*. "It takes time to adjust," she advised. "I'm sure these 'ghillies' are perfectly nice once you get to know them."

The super-popular "ghillies" had been friends for years and existed in their own little bubble. As if anticipating their popularity and good grades, their mothers had given them fashionable names, such as Alicia, Amanda, Allison, etc. What one did, they all did. When Alicia cut her long brown hair so that it grazed her shoulder, the other "A-girls" cut theirs, until the style eventually filtered down to the lower parts of the alphabet. They all wore it in the perfect side "tuck" that accentuated their pierced earrings, usually pearls but sometimes little gold hoops.

When I asked my mother if I could get my ears pierced, she said, "Absolutely not!" She was afraid I'd wind up looking like one of Mosa's relatives, who appeared to have stabbed her lobes with elephant tusks. "You want ears down to your knees—fine," my mother said.

Taking that as a yes, I went with Bumpa to his ear doctor in Lawrence. Bumpa's tinnitus, which he described as a swarm of bees buzzing in his left ear, was getting worse. Apparently, nothing could be done about it. Even though he said it was enough to drive anyone to Danvers, he rarely complained. After the doctor pronounced him "fine, except for the buzzing and partial deafness," Bumpa inquired if he pierced ears. I was afraid the doctor would think it beneath him, but within seconds, he whipped out a piercing gun, and I was wearing tiny gold studs. When I came home, my mother was furious, but by the end of the evening, she'd decided that she wanted pierced ears too.

My gold studs didn't help me fit in any better at school. "You're like a ghillie out of water," my grandfather joked, but it wasn't funny. The students may have been devil worshippers, but they knew their math and science. I'd won the science prize in eighth grade, but that was only because Sister Mary Ethelburger had spread the awards among my girlfriends, and she didn't want to exclude me. I can't even recall the subject of science ever coming up, which left me at a distinct disadvantage now that I was in the advanced class. My teacher, Mr. Bachman, wore the same brown suit every day and wrote indecipherable formulas on a blackboard that we copied into our lab books. On my first report card, he gave me a D.

"Are you making any progress with the ghillies?" Miss Hagenauer would ask before each lesson. I confessed that I didn't have any ghillie friends and hated the new school. She pointed to the picture of a horse-drawn carriage that hung above our piano.

"My grandfather always wanted one of those," she said. "And do you know what he got instead?"

I shook my head no.

"He got a hearse."

"Did he become an undertaker?"

"No, he dropped dead."

"Oh."

I wasn't sure what to make of it. Was it a remnant of a dream she'd been having, or did the story have a moral that applied to me?

"What do you think it means?" I asked my mother.

"I'd say it means that people who expect too much—like you—often wind up . . ."

"In a hearse? Why am I even bothering to take piano lessons, then? You might as well put me in the ground right now."

"Really, Patricia, where do you get your ideas?"

At my mother's next hair appointment, Mrs. Godfrey suggested I take dance lessons from her daughter, Leanne. Dancing, she explained, was the best way to meet people. "But the lessons are private," I told my mother. "Who am I going to meet besides Leanne?"

Leanne had exotic green eyes lined with kohl and a wild mane of multicolored hair. She was going through what my mother referred to as a "hard divorce" and smoked like a fiend. Years earlier, I'd taken tap and ballet at another studio, realizing very quickly that I had no talent. I did, however, love the dancing shoes, especially the patent-leather ones with the bows and metal taps.

"What kind of shoes do I need?" I asked Leanne at my first lesson.

"None."

She explained that with modern dance it was better to go barefoot so you could use your foot's moisture for better balance. "Isadora Duncan and Martha Graham were both advocates of dancing bare-foot," she explained. "Your feet may hurt in the beginning, but over time you'll develop calluses."

Leanne showed me her hardened feet, which looked like she'd danced over fields and meadows, like the heroine of *The Red Shoes*. I didn't want my feet to wind up like hers, but since Leanne liked talking more than teaching, I didn't have to worry. After I performed a few clumsy tendus and chassés, we'd sit in the corner of the studio while she smoked and doled out advice about "rotten" men. I suspected she had a drinking problem. Or maybe she just liked smoking and talking, especially to the students with no talent for dancing. Maybe she was sparing us career heartbreak, since we'd have heart-break enough with all the rotten men in the world.

"Have you ever been in love?" Leanne asked during one of our spontaneous and unsolicited chats.

I thought of Francis What's-His-Name, whose name I'd carry like a secret tattoo for the rest of my life. I thought it better not to mention him since he fell into the "rotten" category.

"Not really."

"Well, don't bother. Look at Isadora Duncan. She had numerous lovers who treated her badly, and then she was strangled."

"By a boyfriend?"

"No, by a scarf."

Leanne was in fact wearing a scarf, and because I didn't want to her to do anything life-threatening with it, I listened to her talk for the rest of my lesson and halfway through the following one. The next student was late and ultimately never showed up. When I finally called my mother, it was dark in the studio. After I left, I imagined Leanne and Isadora Duncan dancing barefoot on their sad callused feet and wondered if their lives would have been happier if they'd taken up tap.

My one consolation was that my friend Agnes hated her school even more than I hated mine, although her issue had nothing to do with bad grades or social cliques. As popular as ever, she'd even started a fashion trend, pairing saddle shoes with nylons. Her complaint was that the nuns at her new school were demanding that all the girls cut their hair. If they didn't comply, the Sister Superior was going to take a pair of scissors to their heads and shear everything off. I explained that all the A-girls at my school had collar-length hair and that it looked great, but accustomed to being an A-girl herself, Agnes dismissed the public school kids as out of step. "I'll look as stupid as Julie Andrews in *The Sound of Music*," she said.

I still loved Julie Andrews and did an excellent impersonation of her singing "My Favorite Things." Agnes knew that, so I thought her comment unnecessarily catty, but I chose to ignore it. She'd recently grown tired of her best friend, Susan, and I sensed a breakup coming on. Though I felt guilty about it, I listened to her complain that Susan was boring and didn't have any original ideas.

Agnes and I spoke on the phone practically every night, dangling our legs off the bed and getting the most awful foot cramps. For some reason, we kind of enjoyed them, especially the way they crept up on us, like an excruciating orgasm, before they culminated in howling pain. "Isn't it against the law for a nun to cut off your hair?" Agnes asked in between screams. "Isn't it personal property?"

As someone all too familiar with the psychic ramifications of having a shorn head, I advised her to seek legal advice. "It's a witch hunt," I said. The pain was so bad I had to jump off the bed and hop around on my foot.

"Stretch your toes, stretch your toes," Agnes yelled through the phone.

We ended the call as we always did, by singing the chorus of the Animals' hit, "We Gotta Get Out of This Place."

Soon we were plotting to do just that. It didn't dawn on us that things might get better and that the nuns wouldn't cut off Agnes's hair or that I wouldn't be friendless forever. It was imperative that we escape our hellish existence before we wound up in Danvers, like our new favorite heroine, Sylvia Plath. Plath actually wound up in Belmont, at McLean Hospital, forty minutes away, but to us it was all the same. We loved Plath for writing tortured poems, such as "Daddy," in which she compared life with her father to living unhappily in a black shoe. We loved her for being a *Mademoiselle* guest editor and marrying a handsome British poet and moving with him to England. We didn't love her for putting her head in an oven, but we understood where she was coming from. She had to get out of that place, if it was the last thing she ever did, and, sadly, it was.

Many of my friends at St. Augustine's had gone to Our Lady of Nazareth Academy in Wakefield, which, unlike Danvers or Peabody, didn't stand for going crazy or shopping. It stood for wicker. Named after Cyrus Wakefield, a former grocer who discovered the many uses of rattan, the town was best known for manufacturing wicker furniture and baskets. When considering high school, I hadn't given it a second thought, but Agnes thought we should transfer to Nazareth. Though she'd be deserting Susan, she confided that she wanted me to be her best friend. That was all I needed.

"You want to do *what*?" my mother said. "Your father won't hear of it." But he did. The minute he got home.

"Patricia wants to go to another school," she yelled from the other side of the powder room, where he'd taken temporary refuge. "It's the craziest thing I've ever heard."

At dinner, I explained that the nuns were going to cut Agnes's hair, and my mother, looking at Nancy, said, "Maybe we should send you to that school."

"And I'm getting D's in science," I added. "I won't be able to get into college."

I started to cry, and fearing that I might wind up in Danvers, my parents relented, and I applied to Nazareth for sophomore year. As long as you were Catholic and could pay the tuition, you were in.

A few weeks before I was set to leave junior high, I looked down at the feet of the A-girl next to me in homeroom. I couldn't believe it, but she was wearing ghillies. "I like your shoes," I whispered. After homeroom, we started talking and she invited me to her house. I worried that it was a trap and that all the A-girls would gang up on me, but she was the only A-girl and it turned out her name started with *C*—for Carol. She said she'd loved my shoes the first day of school, but they didn't sell them at Reinhold's.

"We all wanted to talk to you, but you seemed stuck-up," she explained.

I didn't know what to say. I wasn't stuck-up. I was shy and insecure and had a bad haircut.

"We can all be friends next year," she added.

But we wouldn't be friends because I wasn't going to Andover High. I was going to the Wicker Capital of America, to a mediocre school that took anyone who applied, and I was going there because Reinhold's didn't stock ghillies.

7

A Bully in Brogues

A few weeks before heading to Nazareth, my mother and I went to a "uniform shoe" store that catered to the police, the military, and Catholic schoolgirls. A gray-haired saleswoman presented me with a tie shoe in rigid blue leather. I'd read *Moby-Dick* over the summer and the first thought that popped into my head was *sperm whale*. The shoes, especially in my then size 9, looked massive, with thick soles and a blockheaded mammalian shape.

"Are you sure these are the right ones?" I asked, hoping the saleswoman had given me the "Original Amphibious Navy Boot" by mistake.

"Nope, these are them," she said. "They'll last a lifetime, believe you me."

"They're what we used to call brogues," my mother said back in the car.

Traditionally, brogues were sturdy, stout shoes that originated in

Ireland and Scotland and were ideal for wet, craggy terrain. The leather was perforated to allow for water drainage. Though these didn't have little holes, the word *brogue* perfectly captured their oaf-ish appearance.

"At least they go with your uniform," my mother added.

If you wanted something to complement a shapeless plaid skirt, itchy woolen sweater, and navy blazer with a baseball-size insignia, these were definitely the shoes.

"I hate them," I said.

"Why do you always have to make such a big deal out of things?" my mother said. "No one asked you to transfer to Nazareth, but you had to follow your friend Agnes. So now you're paying the price."

After Labor Day, with a heavy heart and heavier shoes, I joined Agnes and my other St. Augustine's friends at the Nazareth bus stop. It was several doors away from Reinhold's, which was displaying its annual "back-to-school" collection in the window.

In comparison to my brogues, the shoes looked spectacular, and I immediately felt nostalgic for the good old days when I could freely waltz into the store, fight with my mother, and come away with something that didn't scream "sperm whale."

Across the street, I spotted Mary Kay Phinney, whose father owned the TV and stereo store. She was heading to Abbot Academy, the sister school to Phillips, and we were all envious that she'd been accepted. She waved but didn't come over. She was an "Abbot girl" now, and we were practically invisible to her.

Everybody at the bus stop had dark tans from spending the sum-mer slathered in baby oil. It made their teeth look extra white. I'd recently gotten braces on both my uppers and lowers. I'd wanted them for years, but my father was already shelling out a fortune on my regular dental checkups. Even though I brushed regularly, I developed cavities at a rate that defied modern dentistry. I never escaped Dr. Weinstock's chair without having at least eight. Once I had a record fifteen. I'd constantly tell my mother that Dr. Weinstock was crazy, but she'd say that I thought everyone was crazy, which was true, but Dr. Weinstock, with his pronounced lisp, bad toupee, and fondness for the drill and mercury amalgams, was possibly the craziest.

"Oops, another catch," he'd say, poking around with his pick. "I'm afraid it's a cavity, you naughty girl." Later, when *Willy Wonka and the Chocolate Factory* came out, he insisted on performing the movie's theme song—"The Candy Man." *"Who can take a sunrise,"* he'd sing. *"Sprinkle it with dew."* Even with a drill and a wad of cotton in my mouth, he expected me to join in. What kind of sicko dentist sings "The Candy Man" to his patients? Answer: A dentist who's bilking them by filling cavities that never existed. When the scam was exposed, Dr. Weinstock committed suicide and was found in his dentist's chair. He'd either shot or hanged himself. I didn't learn about it until years later, by which time my mother had conveniently forgotten the salient details.

The Nazareth bus driver had to pick up the Lawrence kids first. Just as the Phillips students looked down on us as "townies," we held the Lawrence kids in equally low regard. Though we'd never be so uncharitable as to actually refer to them as our social inferiors, they were city kids, and we lived in an affluent suburb. When the bus finally arrived, Agnes and I made our debut as "best friends" by sharing a seat. Sitting alone was about the worst thing that could happen to a girl, a public declaration that she was a freak and a loner. Though she might pretend that she preferred her own seat, stretching out her legs as if she owned the bus, no one was fooled.

A girl up front was trying to obscure her solo status by flirting with the driver, a wisecracking guy in his early thirties, with greasy, slicked-back hair. The girl was what my mother would have described as "cheap." She'd ironed her dyed-black hair so that it moved in a solid block, and she'd artfully turned her eyebrows into the universal cheap girl shape: the tadpole. With her Yardley silver shimmer lipstick and kohl-rimmed eyes, she looked like a member of a girl gang. While normally I'd have felt bad for someone sitting alone, she didn't elicit an ounce of my sympathy.

Nazareth, or Naz, as all the girls called it, was on thirty acres of woodlands that had once belonged to Charles Newell Winship, a knitwear millionaire. In 1947, Winship's widow sold the property, including a beautiful Georgian Revival mansion, to the Sisters of Charity of Nazareth. Looking to expand their mission beyond their Kentucky home base, they sent one group of nuns to establish a girls' school in Massachusetts and another to open a leprosy clinic in India.

Since I'd never encountered any Southerners before, I initially chalked up the nuns' odd behavior to regional differences. People in Massachusetts call milk shakes frappés, which may sound strange to New Yorkers, so I vowed to be open-minded and perhaps even learn something about the South. But within weeks, I realized that the nuns' strange behavior was nothing like calling milk shakes frappés. You couldn't even call it eccentric, because that would imply a loopy Southern charm, and in no part of the country would these nuns be described as charming.

Our homeroom teacher, Sister Mary Elizabeth, had a flirtatious Blanche DuBois quality that was embarrassingly obvious whenever the school's chaplain came to deliver his weekly lecture. I think it was about sex, but it was hard to know because he spoke in code. One day, he warned us against doing anything to "excite" boys, because we'd be responsible for them "spilling their seed." I'd never heard the phrase before and had no idea what it meant. Did he think we were dating farmers? Sister Mary Elizabeth blushed and had to open a window because she was feeling faint. She then started wearing eye makeup, and while subtly and artfully applied, it did leave you wondering if she'd chosen the right vocation. Eventually, she disappeared. Some heard that she'd had a breakdown, others that she'd been "reassigned" to the leper colony. In any event, nobody really missed her, because there were plenty more like her.

Our English teacher, Sister Patrice was infatuated with a dead priest named Father Magee. She believed that he should be made a saint, even though he'd yet to perform any miracles. That's where she came in. Before every English class, she'd lead us in the following prayer: "Please, Father Magee, send us a million dollars." Who was Father Magee? And why did a nun who'd taken a vow of poverty need a million dollars? She told us that Father Magee had appeared to her in a dream, telling her that the money would rain down from the sky the following Friday. We were in the process of studying *The Scarlet Letter*, and Sister Patrice had chosen Christine, the most beautiful girl in our class, to be Hester Prynne. Christine was a groupie for the Fugs, the satirical rock band that attempted to levitate the Pentagon as a protest against the Vietnam War. The nun's decision to make her stand on top of a desk with a big scarlet *A* on her chest was not purely coincidental.

While Christine read parts of *The Scarlet Letter*, Sister Patrice kept reminding us to pay attention to the story, although hers seemed far more thrilling. What if, like Hester Prynne, she and the priest had a daughter? I wasn't sure where the money factored in, but maybe the girl had become a heroin addict and was mired in debt. With five minutes to go, we couldn't stand it anymore and walked over to the window. The only thing that rained down from the sky was a leaf and a piece of plastic that caught on a tree branch. As Christine removed the scarlet letter from her chest, Sister Patrice fled to the ladies' room. By the end of the semester, she was gone too.

The other students, even my old pals from St. Augustine's, didn't seem to think anything was wrong. Agnes was the only other person who hated the school, but by then she also hated me. I should have seen it coming. Girls who are capable of casting off one best friend will inevitably shed the next. Within several months, Agnes had ditched me for the girl with the ironed hair and silver lips, the one who was no longer sitting solo on the bus. Her name was Joan, and she was a junior.

Since Agnes was partly responsible for why I left my old school, it seemed particularly insensitive of her to dump me so soon after arriving at my new one. I wouldn't have minded as much if she'd dumped me and then moved on to a life of gang violence with Joan, but Agnes couldn't dump a girlfriend without also torturing her. She and Joan sat together on the school bus and whispered about me. They passed mean notes making fun of my braces. In ancient Greece, people painted a representation of their enemy on the soles of their shoes. Agnes and Joan took a different tack. After I told Agnes that I thought our Naz shoes resembled sperm whales, she and Joan began drawing pictures of whales in my textbooks. The drawings were in ink, and I couldn't erase them. Time after time, I'd return to my homeroom to find an increasingly elaborate five-volume illustrated history of *Moby-Dick* under my desk. There were big whales, little whales, whales spouting water, whales with harpoons stuck in their sides.

Commuting to school was torment. Now I was the girl sitting alone, while Agnes and Joan sat behind the driver, giggled, and pointed at me. The ride home was the worst. Joan and some of the other girls had convinced the bus driver to stop every afternoon at a pizza and sub shop on Route 28. By then, it was already four thirty and we were only fifteen minutes from Andover and ninety minutes from dinner. Everybody except me would file out to order pizzas and huge submarine sandwiches and then eat them on the bus. It added another fifteen minutes to our forty-five-minute commute, prolonging my torture as the girl without a best friend or greasy sub.

One day, the Sister Superior called me into her office to let me know that she was aware of my "trial." I thought, *Okay, now she'll put an end to it.* But she said that I should view it as a "test from God" and that I should suffer quietly and with dignity. I'd seen *The Nun's Story* with Audrey Hepburn and found it infuriating when the Mother Superior asked Audrey to fail her medical exams as a show of humility. Eventually, Audrey left religious life, but I couldn't leave Nazareth because I'd only been there a few months.

At the end of sophomore year, Agnes transferred to Andover High School and immediately cut her hair into a geometric bob. Given that she'd left her other school because she wanted to keep her hair long, the irony wasn't lost on me, but at least my "trial" was over. Joan was riding solo again, spending the commute picking at her split ends and licking marinara sauce off her silver lips.

Moby-Dick disappeared for good.

꩜

During the summer between junior and senior years, I joined Andover's new community theater group. I'd hoped Priscilla Lane might make an appearance, but after being a big Hollywood star, it was probably too much of a professional comedown. Only seven or eight people showed up, including two boys around my age, an elderly woman, and an attractive young married couple in their mid-twenties.

The wife had been a theater major at Bennington, where she'd done Shakespeare in the nude or Strindberg in the nude or maybe she was just nude herself. I can't recall all the details. Her husband was a quiet man who wanted to open a bookstore. They seemed headed for divorce.

Due to our small size, we couldn't embark on anything that required a Greek chorus or multitudes of peasants, so Euripides and Chekhov were out. The group's founder, an attractive middle-aged woman who spoke with an Eastern European accent, suggested Edna St. Vincent Millay's one-act play *Aria da Capo*. It featured the traditional commedia dell'arte characters of Pierrot, the melancholy poet, and Columbine, the beautiful amorous ingénue, along with two murderous shepherds and Cothurnus, the Masque of Tragedy. She explained that Cothurnus was not a mythological figure but the name of the high, thick-soled lace boots worn by actors in Greek tragedies. She seemed to be looking in my direction. My Naz shoes had finally found their métier.

The Bennington grad volunteered to direct. She had waist-length brown hair, winged eyeliner, and full lips, and wore dangly ethnic earrings, lots of rings, and shirts with plunging necklines. I hadn't the slightest idea how such an exotic creature wound up in a run-down community center in Andover. Neither, I suspected, did she. "Mrs. Bennington" confessed that she'd vastly prefer to be working "off-off Broadway," and that St. Vincent Millay wasn't Pinter or Beckett or even her freshman-year roommate, who created a whole new kind of theater that involved astrology and Navajo blankets. Nevertheless, she'd do what she could with Pierrot and Columbine, describing them as Punch and Judy types. To my delight and abject fear, she cast me as Columbine. A cute boy named John was Pierrot.

"So, shall we start?" She looked at me.

"Pierre, a macaroon! I cannot *live* without a macaroon!" I said, sounding ludicrously like Katharine Hepburn. I'd recently watched *The Philadelphia Story* and had been practicing her accent. *Oh, Dexter, I'll be yar now, I promise to be yar.*

"John?" Mrs. Bennington said.

"My only love, you are *so* intense! . . . Is it Tuesday, Columbine? I'll kiss you if it's Tuesday."

John had already been accepted to Chicago's Goodman School of Drama and was really talented, because he made me believe that he actually wanted to kiss me. I faked a cough so he wouldn't see me blush. That night I took *Aria da Capo* to bed with me and rehearsed the various ways I could say, "Pierrot, a macaroon! I cannot *live* without a macaroon!" I'd never had a macaroon and wasn't big on sweets, so I'd have to work up an appetite. "Pierrot, a macaroon! I *cannot* live without a macaroon . . . *I* cannot live *without* a macaroon . . . I cannot *liiiiivvvve* . . ."

It didn't take me long to realize that I'd been horribly miscast. Columbine was a joyous, frivolous flirt, and I was none of those things. Though Mrs. Bennington urged me to relax and have fun, I was terrified of making a fool of myself, and since Columbine reveled in her foolishness, I was stuck. I wished they'd selected a more suitable play for my debut, such as Shaw's *Saint Joan*. I was more likely to hear voices and save France than die for want of a macaroon.

John had no problem playing the self-centered, seductive Pierrot, and offstage he could be an awful flirt, reciting Pierrot's lines as if he meant them for real. One night, sneaking up behind me, he whispered, "Let's drink some wine and lose our heads and love one another." I became so flustered I didn't know what to say, until I suddenly remembered the follow-up: "Pierrot, don't you love me now?" From then on, whenever he flirted with me, I'd remind myself that he was only staying in character, and I'd throw Columbine's lines back at him so he'd know I was in on the trick. To make sure he didn't think I actually liked him, I also made a point of treating him badly and being as sarcastic as possible. Yet deep down, I kept hoping that a part of him, the non-actor part, was interested in me, and on the days we didn't rehearse, I longed for him so badly it actually hurt. Though I'd had crushes on Nathan and Francis What's-His-Name, this was different. I could practically feel my chest collapsing under the weight of my own emotions.

Before each rehearsal, Mrs. Bennington led us in a series of relaxation and postural exercises and then directed us to take our places on the stage. John and I sat on high-backed chairs at opposite ends of a long, narrow banquet table and ran through the play. By now it was pretty obvious to everyone that I wasn't a natural-born seductress. I overheard Mrs. Bennington say to her husband, "The girl's a disaster." They even debated getting one of the shepherds to play Columbine. "It could be revolutionary," Mrs. Bennington said. Every time I had to recite the line "I'm *hot* as a spoon in a tea cup," I kept thinking of little Maria Goretti getting stabbed for a macaroon.

While John and I waited backstage for the two murderous shepherds to kill each other, I did a few neck rolls to loosen up. John came up behind me and began rubbing my shoulders. I closed my eyes and tried to give myself over to the sensation. When he finished, he whispered, "My only love, you are *so* intense," which was a line from the play, but then he added, "Can I kiss you?" At that point, I was totally confused. The correct line was "I'll kiss you if it's Tuesday," but it was Monday, so did he still want to kiss me?

"Pierrot, a macaroon," I said, playing it safe. "I cannot *live* without a macaroon."

He took his hands off my shoulders and backed away. "Ah, Columbine," he sighed. "You are *so* literal."

When I got home that night, my mother had skimmed the play and did not like it one bit. "I hope you are not playing that Columbine woman. She's immoral."

"Rest assured I'm not Columbine," I said. It wasn't exactly a lie—my mother could have asked Mrs. Bennington and everyone in the cast and they'd have said the same thing. "I'm the Masque of Tragedy," I added. "A shepherd stabs me at the end because he wants my macaroons."

"Oh, that's fine, then," she said.

With two weeks to go before the performance, Mrs. Bennington took me aside for a "little talk." I figured I was going to get fired.

"Have you ever kissed a boy for a very long time?" she asked.

"Sure," I said, which was definitely a lie.

"And didn't it feel like you just wanted him to rip off your clothes and let him lick you everywhere?"

"Sure."

"So why can't you conjure up that sensual feeling for John? He's awfully sexy."

I didn't know what to say, so I stood there with a stupid look on my face.

"Oh . . . wait a minute," she said. "Don't tell me." She whispered, "You're not attracted to men."

"Why do you say that?"

"*Please.* I went to Bennington. But remember, acting is all about pretending. Can you do that? Can you pretend he's sexy?"

"I'll try."

At the dress rehearsal, I finally saw my outfit, which was made of black-and-white geometric cotton and resembled a Marimekko tablecloth. It started at my neck and ended at my ankles. When I asked Mrs. Bennington why she'd decided to dress me in a strait-jacket, she replied, "The design is very Op art, and besides, we needed to steer clear of décolleté."

Why? Because I had small breasts? Or because she thought I'd freak out if I wore something low-cut?

I asked Bumpa to drive me to Reinhold's so I could at least buy a pair of sexy shoes. Though I had my driver's license, I was petrified of getting behind the wheel. My first time out, I hit a dog, on Easter Sunday, with my mother in the passenger seat. Ultimately, the dog emerged with fewer scars than I. From then on, whenever I attempted to drive, my mother would remind me not to kill any animals, which had the expected inhibitory effect.

Since I couldn't get myself to say the word *sexy* in front of Bumpa, I tried to describe what I wanted in a roundabout way. I must have succeeded, because the salesman presented me with a pair of high-heeled bedroom slippers. Since I didn't want to be taller than John, I managed to mumble, "Sexy but flat." The salesman returned with a pair of shoes that we now call ballerinas but were then known as "the kind of shoes Audrey Hepburn wore." These were cut lower than usual, revealing what is currently referred to as "toe cleavage." "These are definitely sexy," the salesman said admiringly. "They're low on the vamp."

"What's a vamp?" I asked.

"Clara Bow, Theda Bara, Louise Brooks," Bumpa explained, while the salesman pointed to the shoe's front opening. How perfect! I was a vamp with a low vamp.

Though I didn't have cleavage up top, I could have it below. I could be sexy in flats and still be flat. Brilliant!

With the help of my new shoes, I tiptoed out of my shell—or

rather Columbine did, while I went along for the ride. Dazzling John with my shoe-based acting skills, I pranced, preened, and flirted, nuzzling his neck and staring up at him in a totally adoring way. He was literally eating the macaroons out of my hand. "What the hell happened to you?" he asked afterward. "You were great." I didn't tell him about the shoes but instead, quoting Columbine, I laughed and said, "La indeed!—How should I know?"

I told my mother that she shouldn't bother coming to the play because the Masque of Tragedy only had a small role and anyway I died. "Sounds good," she said, chasing Nancy around the living room. I insisted she stay home. "Really, it's not worth your time."

When I got to the theater, John was already in his clown suit and Mrs. Bennington was painting his face white, drawing black triangles around his eyes. Careful not to smudge anything, she fastened the big ruffled collar around his neck and helped him put on a conical-shaped hat. While he waited outside, I slipped on my dress, and Mrs. Bennington, who had a flair for makeup, turned me into a smoldering sexpot. Looking in the mirror, I hardly recognized myself. Then I put on my cleavage-baring flats. La indeed!—The transformation was complete.

As the audience filed in, we took our places at the banquet table, and John toasted me with a glass of Welch's grape juice: "Columbine, my love, you'll be a star by five o'clock." I rolled my eyes. Once we finished the play, I hoped we could have a normal conversation without Edna St. Vincent Millay providing the dialogue for us.

"Here we go," Mrs. Bennington whispered, raising the curtain. I took a deep breath. "Pierrot, a macaroon! I cannot *live* without a macaroon."

John gazed at me with his electrifyingly sexy eyes. "My only love, you are *so* intense." He reached across the table to give me a macaroon and, grabbing his hand, I began nibbling his fingers and soon I was draping my arm around his shoulder, licking his ear, burrowing my head in his wide-ruffled collar. When it came time to say, "I'm hot as a spoon in a teacup!" I made it obviously clear what I was hot for, wriggling my hips and giving the line a Mae West delivery. The audience loved it.

I was starting to relax, forgetting about everybody except Pierrot, who, beneath the clown makeup, seemed totally entranced by me. Modeling my dress for him, I kept twirling around, until I fell purposely across his lap. John was reciting his next line when I caught sight of someone in the audience: my mother.

"My love, by yon black moon, you wrong us both," John said, giving me a little spanking. My mind went blank.

"My love, by yon black moon, you wrong us both," he repeated.

I'd wronged my mother too. By yon black moon, I'd lied! How was I going to convince her that Columbine was also the Masque of Tragedy? By having a total meltdown on stage—that's how!

"There isn't a sign of a moon, Pierrot!" Mrs. Bennington whispered from the wings.

I thought of all the time I'd spent getting into character. I thought of my shoes. Cleavage. *Vamp.*

"There isn't a sign of a moon, Pierrot," I said, getting back into character again. The audience laughed; they thought my temporary amnesia had been part of the play, and from then on, everything went smoothly. The shepherds killed each other, and the Masque of Tragedy shouted, "Strike the scene!" At the end when we came out for our bows, we got a standing ovation and five curtain calls. John kissed my hand, and up until then, except for when I got my ears pierced, it was the single happiest moment of my life.

The group's founder invited everyone back to her house for a cast party. John was already wiping off his makeup, and while I didn't necessarily want a clown for a boyfriend, I didn't want him to revert to being John just yet.

"Are you going to the party?" he asked

I shrugged, as if I had a hot date that night. "I'm not sure. Maybe, maybe not."

I hoped he'd say, "Let's drink some wine and lose our heads and love one another," or the contemporary equivalent, but all he said was, "Well, I guess I'll see you sometime."

"Yeah."

I was too dejected to go to the party, so I went home. I'd completely forgotten about my mother, who was waiting at the kitchen table, looking none too pleased.

"I thought you said you were playing tragedy," she said.

I broke down in tears. "I'm playing it right now. Happy?"

"Pierrot was really cute," she said. "Reminded me of Paul McCartney."

This made me cry even harder, and suddenly Emily and Nancy came running downstairs. They wanted to know what was going on.

"Nothing," my mother said. "She just experienced a tragedy, but she'll get over it."

"What kind?" Emily asked. "Did somebody die?"

"Yes," I said. "I did. Inside."

"You know what you need right now?" my mother said. "Macaroons!"

"I never want to hear the word *macaroon* again!"

"Well, you won't because we don't have macaroons in the house anyway."

"*Macaroons, macaroons, macaroons,*" Emily and Nancy began chanting.

I went to bed, while they ate Oreos. All I could think of was that in a couple of weeks, John would be in Chicago, and I'd never see him again. I was heartsick. No, *crushed*.

Postscript: I did see him again—three decades later. By then he'd had an impressive stage career and had been nominated for a Tony. He was then appearing in a TV drama with my friend Glynnis, who knew the background story and mentioned my name to him. "He told me that he'd really liked you," she explained, "but you were cold and sarcastic. He thought you hated him."

Several weeks later, we had lunch together—salad, coffee, no macaroons—and by yon black moon, we were both now married and middle-aged, and the play seemed like a lifetime ago.

⁂

By senior year, I'd fully accepted that going to Naz was like going to Danvers. Sister Alberta, our ancient English teacher, was too tired to conduct class, but managed to work around the issue by convincing us that we were too tired to learn. After instructing us to put our heads down on our desks and "rest," she read to us, as if we were still in kindergarten. She preferred Southern writers with a flair for the macabre. Her favorite short story was Faulkner's "A Rose for Emily," about a reclusive Southern spinster who feeds her lover rat poison and then cohabits with his corpse. After she finished reading it, she didn't call for a class discussion because the class was asleep. I thought I'd enliven things by asking if the story was about necrophilia, but Sister Alberta said, "Just put your head down on your desk, dear, and it will be over soon."

In addition to the nuns, we had several lay teachers, including Mrs. Barnett, who taught drama and speech. She was pretty and smart, and because she wasn't insane, I adopted her as my role model.

Some of the other students criticized her for using a depilatory on her mustache. Since I'd never heard the term *depilatory*, one of the Italian girls explained that Mrs. Barnett's upper lip was red every week before speech class—a sure giveaway that she was using something to get rid of excess hair. She began calling her Mrs. Depilatory. Given the stunted education at Naz, Mrs. Barnett's mustache seemed a refreshing symbol of growth. I began taking private drama lessons with her after school.

With Mrs. Barnett's encouragement I become president of the drama club and starred in a play about nurses who become addicted to heroin. I overdosed in the end, performing what I thought was a brilliant death scene. Since the nuns were preoccupied with staging our spring musical—*Flower Drum Song*—they hadn't paid any attention to the content of the play and when they finally saw it, I was called into Sister Superior's office.

"A play about a drug addict?" she said. "Have you totally lost your mind?"

After I told her that the nurse died for her sins, she was somewhat pacified until she noticed I was wearing mascara. "Take that off immediately!" she said. "Next you'll be wearing eye shadow and rouge, and then what?" In her mind, mascara was a gateway cosmetic that would inevitably lead to an acting career and depilatory addiction.

The spring dance was the final event before commencement, and I didn't have a date. Mrs. Barnett fixed me up with her nephew, who went to Phillips and who came from a prominent Andover real estate family. The other girls were going with boys from the local Catholic prep schools, or ones heading off to the military or possibly jail. I needed a dress, a really great one. My mother, acknowledging the importance of the occasion, took me to Yankee Lady, a small boutique off Main Street. It sold preppy Lily Pulitzer–type prints and

other emblems of the WASP lifestyle. For years the store's most cov-
etable item had been a straw fishing tackle bag with a long leather
strap. I wanted it more than anything, and when Bumpa bought it
for me, I was thrilled.

The saleswoman wore her steel-gray hair in a chin-length bob and
spoke in an affected accent. I'd carried my straw bag to show that I
wasn't just any non–Yankee Lady who'd walked in off the street.

"She needs a dress for the spring dance," my mother said.

"Oh, at Phillips?" the saleswoman asked.

"No," I said.

She was nosy and wouldn't let it go. "So *where?*"

"Nazareth," I mumbled.

"Isn't that in the Holy Land?"

"It's in Wakefield," my mother explained. "She's dating a Phillips
boy." She casually dropped his name, and the saleswoman immediately perked up.

"Oh," she said, smiling. "Then you need something very special."

I tried on numerous dresses, each worse than the last. I wasn't the
Lily Pulitzer type. Finally, the saleswoman showed me a long dress
covered in tropical splashes of fuchsia and lime. It reminded me of
the gowns Oleg Cassini had designed for Jackie Kennedy, if Jackie
had been color-blind and forced to attend a black-tie luau.

"That really brightens her up, don't you think?" the saleswoman
said to my mother, who agreed. She was tired of looking at dresses.

The store carried a small selection of shoes, and the saleswoman
said she had a perfect match. She presented me with a pair of patent-
leather heels in a brilliant shade of ruby. It wasn't a color I'd normally
wear, but the dress wasn't something I'd normally wear. Going to a
formal dance wasn't something I normally did, and going on a date
was something I never did. All in all, it was virgin territory.

Mrs. Barnett's nephew turned out to be adorable, with dark brown hair and eyes and the cutest smile. He was sweet and polite and never complained when the nuns kept a vigilant watch on our dancing, making sure the boys weren't spilling their seeds on our new dresses, resulting in mortal sin and costly dry cleaning. Afterward, he drove me home, kissed me good night, and never called again. It was obvious that he was only doing his aunt a favor, and that was okay. I had my ruby slippers, and I'd go wherever they'd take me.

8

To Oz and Back

The shoes took me to Washington, DC, where I spent my freshman year at the Catholic University of America. I know what you're thinking, that by now I should have tried something different, like a yeshiva, or even the Pontifical Catholic University of Rio de Janeiro, where according to the school's brochure, little monkeys jump among the trees. But the Catholic University of America had one thing the Catholic University in Rio did not and that was a great drama department with teachers who spoke English. I'd read that several famous actors had attended the school, including Jon Voight, who played Rolf in the original Broadway production of *The Sound of Music*. That was enough for me.

I wore my ruby shoes the first day of class, pairing them with lime-green culottes, matching vest, and a polyester fuchsia shirt from Casual Corner at the Peabody mall. It was 1969. Neon colors were in. If you ignored the actual outfit, I could have stepped out of a Peter

Max poster. The CU campus was large, the pumps uncomfortable. After two days of walking, I developed a blister, which turned into an abscess, and I landed in the infirmary for a week. My foot needed to be soaked and drained several times a day and didn't appear to be improving.

"Am I going to lose my foot?" I asked the nurse, who was also a nun.

She pointed to the pearl ring Bumpa had given me as a high school graduation present. "Do your parents approve?"

"Why wouldn't they?"

"You're very young to be walking down the aisle."

"So I'll be able to walk?"

"Marriage is a big commitment, and I don't think you're ready."

"I don't think so either."

"So maybe you should break off the engagement."

It finally occurred to me that she'd drawn the wrong conclusion from my ring, possibly imagining that some sweet Rolf type had seduced me in an Alpine gazebo, while singing "Sixteen Going on Seventeen." After setting her straight, she went on and on about how young girls are often led astray their first year of college.

"Am I going to be able to walk again?"

"What a silly question! Of course you are!"

And I did. After three semesters, I walked out of Catholic University, just as Jon Voight left the von Trapps to become a Nazi and later a hustler in the Oscar-winning *Midnight Cowboy*. Well, not exactly like that, but I did take my ruby slippers and got out of there.

"You want to do *what?*" my mother said when I brought up the idea of transferring. "I can't even mention this to your poor father. He will have an absolute fit." Over the years, my father had gone from someone who had "plenty" to say, even though he was very quiet, to someone prone to "fits," even though he rarely lost his temper. I patiently explained my reasons for wanting to leave, including the lack of diversity among the student population. "I think it would be good for me to go to school with people other than just Catholics," I said. As expected, that didn't go over too well, so I skipped to the next reason. CU was in the northeastern part of DC, adjacent to a crime-ridden neighborhood. Several female students had been raped and we couldn't walk unaccompanied to the library at night. Three of my girlfriends were transferring to other schools.

"So what are you saying?" my mother asked.

"That I could be raped and murdered."

I didn't have to add, "Do you want that on your conscience?" because we were both geniuses at inducing guilt.

"Well, okay," she said finally. "But if your father has a coronary from the stress, it will be on your conscience."

There's no place like home. I wound up at Tufts University, in Medford, which is a mere fifteen minutes from Andover. Emily had moved into my bedroom and was now the Big Sister, a role she achieved by wearing platform shoes that made her even taller than her height of five feet nine. She had several pairs, including espadrilles and a cork wedge-heel platform from the popular brand Kork-Ease. I had to look up to her whenever we spoke, which, as a middle child, was undoubtedly the desired effect. Despite our age difference, we'd grown closer in recent years, bonding one summer during long walks along the beach. We shared a similar sense of humor and laughed at the same things.

At the time, Nancy wasn't into shoes or fashion at all. At least she'd agreed to brush her hair, which my mother considered a milestone of child development, although it was not without its trade-offs. Nancy demanded to eat her dinners in front of the TV in the basement/den. This was not a particular hardship for my mother. In many ways, it was easier having her out of the way, but my mother pretended it was a sacrifice she was willing to make for the sake of appearances, specifically Nancy's. While Bumpa prepared the evening meal, Nancy would descend into the basement to watch reruns of *Gilligan's Island*, singing the theme song at the top of her lungs. Bumpa would say, "That's wonderful, dear!" and then she'd demand hors d'oeuvres, and he'd bring down Cracker Barrel cheese on Ritz crackers. Dinner on a tray would follow.

Around the same time, Nancy rescued a kitten from a "Save a Pet" booth at a local school fair. She hadn't bothered to consult my mother. After much back-and-forth, including the usual tears, screaming, and threats to run away, Nancy was allowed to keep the cat, which she named Pie. The two were inseparable; she enjoyed dressing it in her doll's clothes, stuffing its arms and legs into a variety of soigné dresses that it wore around the house and inside the litter box. She also taught it to do somersaults, throwing aluminum foil balls at the ceiling, while Pie jumped eight feet off the ground, twirled in the air, and then executed a perfect landing on the oriental carpet.

With the flying cat and numerous other distractions, I was happy that I'd made the decision to board at Tufts, where I was assigned a double room in a dormitory suite. As a transfer student, I didn't have a choice of roommates and mine was either suffering from severe depression or else she hated me. Possibly both. She was addicted to playing James Taylor's "Fire and Rain," and while I realize there are worse addictions, this one was pretty bad. "Fire and Rain" is a beautiful song. It's also about depression, substance abuse, and suicide. It doesn't leave you feeling happy, the way you might after listening to the Partridge Family. I'm not saying I liked the Partridge Family, but after a steady diet of "Fire and Rain," David Cassidy took on qualities that we now ascribe to Prozac.

Across the hallway were two pretty, perky girls, who were both engaged to frat boys and were always having the kind of fun I associated with being a coed in a 1950s musical. A senior with long blond hair lived in the single at the end of the hallway. I remember her as a hippie but that may have been only in comparison to the coeds. She spent her free time smoking pot and concocting various conspiracy theories on why Paul McCartney was dead, even though Paul McCartney had stated publicly that he was very much alive. With the coeds off doing fun things, like going on hayrides and my roommate reliving James Taylor's experience at the Austen Riggs psychiatric facility, I hung out with the hippie, listening to her play "Revolution 9" backward a million times.

"He's saying, 'Turn me on, dead man,'" she explained. "Isn't that proof enough?"

She'd then move on to "Strawberry Fields Forever," the song that she and millions of other conspiracy theorists claimed was definite proof that Paul was dead. John supposedly uttered the words, "I buried Paul," when he actually said "cranberry sauce." Next she'd usually pull out the *Abbey Road* cover, which showed the Beatles walking across the street. "Isn't it just like a funeral procession?" she'd ask. "John's wearing white, so he's the priest. Ringo is in black, so he's the undertaker, and George is in jeans, so he's the grave digger. Paul is barefoot, so that means he's dead."

"I'm not sure going barefoot means you're dead," I said, although I knew better than to challenge her because she'd practically majored in "Paul Is Dead."

"Did you know that in the Kabbalah the body is described as the shoe of the soul?" she asked. "What do shoes do?" She didn't wait for an answer. "They protect your feet from rocks and splinters and dirt. In the same way, the body acts as a shoe to protect the soul from our dirty physical world."

"And that means Paul is dead?"

I was beginning to wonder if Tufts was really for me. My suite mates were weird, all in different ways, and in a repeat of what had happened when I'd left St. Augustine's for Andover Junior High, I'd gone from getting straight A's to receiving average grades. Some of my teachers' comments were lacerating. "You are the worst writer I have ever encountered," an esteemed Shakespeare scholar noted on one of my papers. "And I am very old." My favorite, though, came from my American Theater professor, referring to a paper I'd written on Ethel Barrymore. After I'd mentioned that she'd gained seventy-five pounds, surely not an insignificant development for an actress, he wrote, *"Now, Patricia, I'm beginning to get annoyed. This tittle-tattle may be good enough for* True Confessions, *but it comes close to character assassination!"*

Midway through the semester, I had a plan. Tufts had a program in London for English and theater majors. Maybe I'd be happier there.

I brought it up to my parents when I was home one weekend. "I'm not sure Tufts-in-Medford is right for me," I told my mother before Sunday dinner. "But I think Tufts-in-London would be perfect. I've always wanted to go to London, and your mother was born in London, and, well, for lots of reasons I think I should be in London."

"For lots of reasons I think you should be in Danvers!" she said. "You better not tell your father, because he will have an absolute fit. His head will explode, and you'll be left to pick up all the pieces.

What is wrong with you? Why can't you just find a place and stay put?"

"Nobody stays in one place anymore."

"Thank you, Carole King," my mother said. I had to hand it to her. She was no slouch when it came to popular culture.

"Well, *you* bring it up to your father. I'm through. But if anything happens to him, if he dies of a coronary and slumps right over the chicken with sherry sauce that Bumpa made especially for you, then don't come crying to me. You brought it on yourself."

I went into the living room, where my father was reading *The Boston Globe.* He loved Sundays because the paper had multiple sections. With Nancy's cat flying over his head, I laid out the plan, including the comparable tuitions. Pie had never achieved such heights before and Nancy called Bumpa in from the kitchen to watch.

"Incredible," Bumpa said, applauding. "Pie is ready for the Olympics."

"By the way, don't forget my hors d'oeuvres," Nancy said. "Besides the cheese and crackers, I'd also like celery sticks filled with cream cheese. But please remove the pimentos."

"It's Sunday," my mother said. "You are not watching TV downstairs."

"So can I go to London?" I asked my father.

"Can I go to London?" Nancy asked.

"At the rate Pie's going, she'll get to London before any of you," Bumpa said, cheering the cat on.

"Okay," my father said. Pie had landed on his lap, obscuring his view of the paper. If he wanted to read the editorials, the cat had to leave and so did I.

Emily was sad when she heard the news. Even though she didn't want me back in the house, she also didn't want me out of the country. I was her closest ally in the family. I felt a twinge of guilt, but how could I not go to London?

When I returned to Tufts that evening, I shared my new plans with my roommate. It may have been the first conversation we ever had. She told me that London was where James Taylor first started writing "Fire and Rain." I immediately left to find the hippie. She was distraught because after much soul-searching and consultation with the campus mental health service, she'd come to the tragic conclusion that Paul was in fact alive.

"Maybe you need to move on," I suggested gently. "I'm going to London."

"To Abbey Road?" She was having a hard time letting go.

"Maybe."

"Remember what the Kabbalah says."

"Wear shoes so people won't think you're dead."

"Yes, and watch out for rocks and splinters."

9

Love on a Shoestring

I fell in love for the first time at Stonehenge. Bending down to lace up one of my new granny boots, I noticed him bending down to tie one of his rust suede shoes. In front of the world's most famous prehistoric monument, we forged a bond based on mutual attraction and loose laces. He gave me a soulful look and said, "Hi." He may have also declared his undying love, but right then a swarm of Girl Scouts descended from a convoy of tour buses and drowned him out. I had a knot in one of my laces and he helped me undo it. His name was Scott, and with his wild mane of curly hair and large blue eyes, he reminded me of Roger Daltrey.

We were touring England as part of the Tufts-in-London program, but instead of taking in the sights, we'd been taking in each other. At Oxford's Bodleian Library, I looked up from the illuminated manuscripts to see him staring at me from across the display case. Walking down one of countless regal staterooms, past portraits of homely royals, I saw him looking past the duchess with the double chin and priceless pearls and directly at me. We didn't say a word. We just looked and then looked away. Finally, after our shoe-tying ceremony at Stonehenge, an ancient Druid rite that transformed us into a couple, we sat together on the bus. Cat Stevens's "Moon Shadow" was playing on the radio. "So, where are you from?" he asked.

In London we lived at a funky South Kensington hotel that served as the school's academic base. By chance, Scott had been assigned the room directly opposite mine. We took most of our classes in the hotel's Victorian parlor rooms, lounging on threadbare sofas and chairs. The hotel had only one tiny shower, and on Saturday nights— theater night—there'd be a line of students clad only in towels, snaking down several flights of stairs. There was so much to see: Laurence Olivier in *Long Day's Journey into Night;* Diana Rigg in Tom Stoppard's *Jumpers;* Peter Brook's *A Midsummer Night's Dream;* Vanessa Redgrave in *The Threepenny Opera;* Alan Bates in *Butley;* Nureyev and Fonteyn in *Swan Lake.* Scott, who wanted to be a composer, introduced me to jazz, and we heard Ornette Coleman, Oscar Peterson, Bill Evans, all the greats. The tickets were so inexpensive we had money left over to eat at cheap Italian restaurants with white tablecloths and candles in Chianti bottles. One night, over a plate of spaghetti carbonara, Scott called me radiant. I said, "It's just the candles and your second beer," but he assured me, "No, it's definitely you."

I wore my granny boots practically every day. They were my "first love" boots. All I had to do was look at them, and I'd feel a surge of happiness that practically made me dizzy. Letters to my parents overflowed with excitement and the occasional odd detail: "My kidneys are fine!" I exulted. "I think I must have gone to the bathroom so frequently at home out of sheer boredom because I haven't had any trouble here. That's what happens when you are HAPPY!"

One day, Nathan, my adolescent crush from the November Club, appeared in Scott's room. It turned out that he was a friend of Scott's roommate and had just returned from Africa. He didn't remember me at all.

"We went to the November Club," I reminded him. "We danced together and then you called me Scarecrow."

"Why would I call you a scarecrow?" he asked, puzzled.

"Especially since she's a cow," added Scott's dreadful roommate, who hated that Scott and I were in love. In truth, I was more cow than scarecrow. I'd gained fifteen pounds devouring Marriott Hot Shoppe cheeseburgers at Catholic University and was no longer thin. But I preferred to think Nathan didn't recognize me, not because a decade had elapsed, or because I'd gained weight, but because love had transformed me beyond all recognition.

During our monthlong winter break, Scott and I made plans to travel together.

My roommate, Barbara, a sweet, easygoing girl from Rhode Island, reminded me how lucky I was to be seeing the world with someone I loved. I agreed. I was very, very lucky.

A few weeks before we were set to go, Scott announced that his father wanted him home for the holidays and had already sent him a plane ticket to New York. I was distraught in a way that's only acceptable when you're young and in love for the first time. A month seemed like a thirty-year jail sentence. I didn't know how I'd be able to handle it. I pictured myself collapsing on the floor, tugging at his corduroy pants, and screaming, "Please don't leave!" In acting class, when our teacher asked us to evoke a painful memory, I remembered the moment when Scott told me he'd be going to New York, and I actually made myself cry. "I didn't think you had it in you," the teacher said. "Brava!"

With my plans canceled, I tagged along with Barbara, her best friend, Caroline, and Mary Sue, who was from Louisiana and wore false eyelashes and a fur stole. Unlike Barbara and Caroline, sensible English majors carrying backpacks, Mary Sue and I were aspiring actresses and traveled with a complete wardrobe. Among Mary Sue's many pieces of luggage was a professional makeup case that had multiple drawers for her lashes, tubes of glue, and dozens of shadows and lipsticks. I brought clothes for every occasion, including ones I was unlikely to attend, such as a papal audience or dinner at a palazzo. Naturally, I brought my granny boots, which I hoped would comfort me during the dark days ahead.

We traveled everywhere by train, standing nose to nose with other passengers for ten hours at a time. Our hotel in Rome had stained wallpaper and a broken toilet that coughed up murky brown water. It rained nearly every day. Italian men, none of whom appeared to own palazzi or even *appartamenti*, followed us everywhere, grabbing, pinching, and making lewd noises. I missed Scott. Nothing compared to the pleasure of his company, not the Sistine Chapel, not the Coliseum, not the "genuine Feragamo" ballet flats that subsequently fell apart because I didn't know how to spell *Ferragamo*.

After Rome, we went to Florence, arriving at the Santa Maria Novella train station, where a cute young policeman asked if we needed a hotel room. He told us that his cousin owned a cheap but charming place around the corner. Figuring he planned to rape us, I whispered my concerns to Barbara, who said, "For God's sake, he's a policeman!" So we went to the hotel, which was indeed clean and charming, and I felt slightly better, until he asked us to have dinner at another cousin's restaurant. He'd bring three other policemen.

They were cousins too. None spoke English, so the conversation was limited, but the food was the best we'd had in Italy. Even better, it was on the house. The next night, we all went to a noisy club, where at some point the first policeman asked me if I wanted to rent a car and see Tuscany with him. After I declined, he turned to Mary Sue, who, batting her false eyelashes, drawled, "Why, sir, you insult me." At the end of the evening, the policeman announced that someone had stolen his wallet and would we mind paying the cover charge and drinks?

The next morning, Barbara took off with him. When she returned several days later, she was flush with excitement. Though she didn't come out and say it, I suspected she'd slept with him. I hoped it wasn't her first time. The next day, we were heading to Venice, and he was supposed to meet us at the train station to return Barbara's rental deposit. He'd dropped off the car himself.

"You know she's never going to see that money," Mary Sue whispered as we waited at the station.

I knew it. Barbara's best friend knew it. But Barbara, even after he'd missed the appointed rendezvous by an hour, even after we'd missed our train, still didn't know it.

"Maybe something's happened to him," she said. "Maybe he got into an accident."

An hour passed, then another. Watching the dawning realization on Barbara's face was excruciating. "He's not coming, is he?" she cried. We all shook our heads no. "He took my money. It's everything I have."

We called the hotel, but the owner claimed he didn't know his cousin's name. Finally, we went to the police station. "One of your policemen stole money from me," Barbara explained. She went through the whole story; by the time she was midway through, we'd attracted an audience of about a dozen policemen who couldn't contain their laughter. None of them spoke much English, but having heard similar stories before, they didn't need to. "Crook," the police chief said. "Thief. *Capisci?*"

Barbara was devastated and hardly spoke for the rest of the trip. I couldn't imagine possibly losing your virginity to a crook. It was bad enough losing your boyfriend to his father. We visited more churches, with their flickering candles, dank musty smells, and dark paintings of skewered martyrs. We ate plates of mediocre spaghetti carbonara, and then, finally, we returned to London, where Scott was waiting for me.

In mid-January, the miners went on strike, and for seven weeks we had intermittent power and electricity. It was thrillingly romantic. We ate our meals and read D. H. Lawrence by candlelight. After one of my teachers read a paper I'd written on *Women in Love,* he suggested I switch from theater to English. And so I decided to become a writer. Mostly, though, I was a woman in love. I lost my appetite and with all the walking we did, I also shed the extra fifteen pounds, plus another five. By the spring, I'd covered so much ground that the local cobbler couldn't do any more repairs on my crumbling granny boots. "These old girls have had a good run," he said, "but they're totally knackered." Scott offered to buy me a new pair of shoes, so we went shopping together on Kensington High Street. He picked out a sensible pair of knockoff Hush Puppies.

"I really like these," he said.

"You mean, for you?"

"No, for you. You need a comfortable pair of walking shoes. Besides, I was getting pretty sick of those granny boots."

"I'd die before I'd wear these," I said.

This escalated into a huge fight. I started to cry, and he walked out of the store, and the salesman, looking uncomfortable, said, "Do you want the shoes or not?" I told him to put them away and I waited for Scott to return. Twenty minutes went by, and no Scott. I couldn't believe he'd leave me in a discount shoe store. Finally, he came back and I was so nervous about losing him that I apologized and let him buy me the $12 knockoff Hush Puppies. They were rust suede—the same color as his shoes. We were a perfect match.

With the school year about to end, Scott hatched a plan to keep us together for the summer. His father was president of a publishing company, and I was offered a temporary job at one of his magazines. His parents agreed to let me stay with them in their New York apartment. What could be more perfect than that? According to my parents, lots of things, starting with a job in Andover. This precipitated a flurry of letters in which I pleaded my case as ardently as Portia in *The Merchant of Venice*. In response to their concern that I was becoming too dependent on Scott, I wrote, *"I am not depending on him for my livelihood, only my happiness, and if wanting happiness counts as an offense, then I, along with the whole human race, plead 'Guilty!'"* Letting me live in New York with my Jewish boyfriend was clearly preferable to reading any more of my letters, so they ultimately gave in.

When I arrived back home, however, my mother quickly made it clear she was not happy. "You should have never left Catholic University," she said. "You've become unchaste and immoral."

I pulled out my precious beat-up granny boots, intending to store them in a safe place. My mother told me to throw them out. "They're filthy and falling apart," she said.

"I fell in love in these boots," I said.

"Well, they look it," she replied.

My mother hated clutter and was famous for tossing things away, even things she wanted to keep, like her diamond engagement ring. "I just want to pitch and chuck everything," she'd say when she was in a spring-cleaning mode that encompassed all seasons. Bumpa cringed whenever she walked past his room and hid his valuables on the top shelf of his closet, above his wooden roller and magic liniment. I placed my granny boots in a plastic bag and asked him if I could store them in his closet.

By the time I was ready to leave for New York, my mother wasn't speaking to me, and I was totally distraught, torn between seeking her approval and wanting independence. Nancy, who was ten, pleaded with me to stay. "You're always leaving us," she said. "I hardly know you." Emily sided with me. If I returned for the summer, she'd have to room with Nancy, but she also thought Scott was adorable and how could I possibly not want to be with him?

My father and Bumpa drove me to the train station. They weren't thrilled with me either, but didn't say anything. I felt as if I'd let everybody down, but it was a job. In New York . . .

♯

Scott was waiting for me in the lobby of his building when I stepped out of the cab. As I gave him a shy kiss in front of the doorman, he muttered something about "complications." While we were falling in love, his parents were falling out of it, and his father wanted a divorce. "He's left my mother for someone else," he explained. "She's a secretary at the company."

"How old is she?" I asked.

"Old," he said. "Thirty-five." His parents, like mine, were in their early fifties.

Scott assured me everything was fine. His father had already moved out and his mother was coping fairly well. The apartment, which was on Sutton Place, was beautiful, with a water view and modern art on the walls. It smelled of cigarettes and something else—alcohol? His mother was in the kitchen crying while doing the *New York Times* crossword puzzle in ink. I noticed a half-empty bottle of Scotch on the counter. After I gave her the box of Russell Stover chocolates I'd bought as a hostess gift, she showed me to my room, which was next to hers. In a gravelly voice, she kept referring to her husband as "that bastard" or alternately "that shit." Sometimes he was the "shit-bastard." She was a genius at profanity combination.

As I unpacked my bag, I told myself that maybe I'd caught her on a bad day. But there were no good days. It was sad, because even at her worst, she was beautiful and brilliant; she'd wanted to be a sculptor but had devoted her life to her husband. Now she was bitter and resentful. Whether she'd always been that way, or if her husband's infidelity had brought out those qualities, I couldn't tell. But without the "bastard" around, she took out her frustrations on her son, whose only crime was being young and in love.

I didn't fare much better. One day, eyeing a magenta peasant blouse I'd bought at Bloomingdale's, she said, "Black is a better color for you." Though she was in mourning for her life, and I was freshly in love, her unhappiness was contagious. At night I'd hear her crying in her room, and I'd want to cry too.

After Scott and his mother got into a major fight, we decamped to his father's apartment on Beekman Place. It had even better views of the river, and Greta Garbo lived around the corner. I was in real estate heaven, but I missed our life in London. We began to argue. One evening, after too much wine, I brought up what his mother had said about his father, that for a publisher, it was strange that he didn't own any books. Scott didn't read much either. I saw a disturbing pattern. Things escalated, and I ran into the bathroom, slamming the door so hard we couldn't open it. The super had to take the door off the hinge. I was dressed only in a towel. The next day, his father told us the building management wanted us out. We repacked our bags and returned to Sutton Place, where his mother didn't even look up from the crossword puzzle.

That night, Scott reminded me that in a couple of days he'd be leaving for two weeks to take a Red Cross lifesaving course in New Hampshire. He'd mentioned it earlier, but I'd conveniently blocked it out. He explained that his father thought it was important to have something to fall back on, in case he didn't make it as a composer. "And *lifeguard* is your next-best option?" I shouted. Later, when Scott said good-bye, I thought he looked less like Roger Daltry and more like his father.

With Scott gone, his mother and I hardly spoke to each other, although by then we had a big thing in common: Our men had abandoned us. She downed Scotch, while I drowned in self-pity. I bought a knockoff Saint Laurent suit in my new favorite color—black. She arranged a face-lift. At night, I'd walk across the street and sit in the same romantic spot Woody Allen would later make famous in *Manhattan*. With the lights of the 59th Street Bridge glittering overhead, I'd stare into the East River and imagine jumping into it. Scott would have to live with the guilt of knowing that while he'd been administering CPR to an inflatable dummy, I'd drowned off the coast of Sutton Place.

Somehow I made it through the rest of August, while Scott earned his lifesaving certificate. Before we returned to Tufts for senior year, I bought a pair of platforms at Alexander's department store. They looked nothing like my granny boots and I towered over Scott.

⁑

After graduation, Scott stayed in Boston to study jazz, while I wrote for the *Lawrence Eagle-Tribune* before moving to New York to get a master's degree in Cinema Studies at NYU. We decided that the separation would be good for us, though we agreed not to date other people. I lived with two other women on East 9th Street, where we paid $500 a month for a six-room apartment with two massive terraces in a doorman building. With another NYU film student, I'd go to the Bleecker Street Cinema or the Little Carnegie, sitting through weeklong festivals of Bergman and Buñuel films. We thought nothing of seeing a double feature of *The Seventh Seal* and *Wild Strawberries,* and then catching the latest Antonioni or Bertolucci. Everybody was taking about "cinema" in those days, and in Manhattan alone, there were dozens of art houses and revival theaters, most of which are now closed.

When Scott finished school in Boston, he moved back to New York, where we rented a studio on East 58th Street, not far from his mother's apartment. I lied and told my mother I was living alone. I don't think she believed me, but unless I initiated the phone calls, I rarely heard from her. It was not an easy time. Some of the tenants staged a rent strike to protest lack of services, and in retaliation, the landlord shut off the power and electricity. What had been romantic in London was dreadful in New York, where we were no longer carefree students with unlimited theater tickets but publishing drones at Scott's father's company. Scott worked as an editorial assistant at a music magazine, while I proofread hotel descriptions for a travel directory, sharing a cubbyhole with a young woman who wanted to be an artist and spent her evenings creating tiny dollhouses.

Several evenings a week, to break up the monotony and to escape my cold, dark apartment, I took jazz at Alvin Ailey. I was a total klutz, but the class attracted interesting people. *Vogue* had recently published a controversial Deborah Turbeville photograph showing a group of models in a bathhouse that suggested a concentration camp. One of the models was in my dance class, and I loved her frizzy hair, so I got a perm. Another model in my class was wearing a pair of Earth shoes, which a Danish yoga instructor had created after noticing the perfect posture of the Brazilian aborigines. Attributing their alignment to walking barefoot in sand, she constructed a shoe with a negative heel that elongated the spine. My Earth shoe phase lasted until Scott's mother said, "What the hell are you wearing on your feet?" As for the frizzy hair, I was stuck with it.

※

The 1970s offered a wide diversity of shoe styles, from negative heels to six-inch glitter platforms. With the women's movement raising the issue of sexism, shoes made a political statement, with some feminists associating high heels with the male-dominated view of women as sex objects. Rather than capitulate to society's attempts to keep women immobile, they opted for Earth Shoes, combat boots, or sensible walking shoes. At the same time, other women, even those who identified with feminism, embraced platforms and Charles Jourdan's sexy "cigarette" heels.

Women were being pulled in several different directions, as evidenced in Scott's own family. His mother, an ardent liberal, began working at Planned Parenthood, while his stepmother focused on decorating her new Park Avenue apartment in shades of white and cream. The ultimate shiksa—a word I'd recently added to my growing Yiddish vocabulary—she was blond, cute, and athletic, with a passion for Lotte Berk workouts, do-it-yourself découpage, and Karl Lagerfeld in his Chloé period.

Right before Christmas, Scott's father invited us to the holiday party he was throwing for his publishing friends. Knowing I was interested in getting a writing job, he urged me to make the rounds and introduce myself. As I've always done when I'm nervous, I went shoe shopping, this time at B. Altman, which was located on Fifth Avenue and 34th Street, a few blocks from the publishing company. It was the only place I had a charge card. First I picked out a simple jewel-neck sweater in black, a black A-line skirt, and a pair of black pumps. The shoes reminded me of the ones Jackie Kennedy had worn to JFK's funeral and suddenly I had the terrible thought that I, too, would be wearing the shoes to a funeral.

The next morning, waking up at six A.M., I nudged Scott and told him to hold me. "Something terrible is going to happen," I said. A few minutes later, I received a call from my father telling me that Bumpa had suffered a massive heart attack the day before. He'd made pancakes for the family, and after finishing up the dishes, he'd climbed back into bed and died. The last time I'd seen him was over the Thanksgiving holiday. He and my father had driven me to the train station, and after they walked me to the platform, I kissed them both good-bye. My father didn't look back, but Bumpa turned around and we waved to each other. I walked a few feet and turned around again. Bumpa did the same thing. It was one of those freeze-frame moments you never forget.

I immediately flew home to Boston, where my father met me at the Eastern Airlines terminal. In an uncharacteristic show of intimacy, he put his arm around me, which made me feel even worse. Things were obviously very bad. We drove to Andover just as the snow was beginning to fall. It would soon turn into one of the biggest blizzards in Boston's history, with a snowfall of eighteen inches. The wake was held at Lungren Funeral Home, not far from Reinhold's, which was now closed. With all the snow, I couldn't wear my new black pumps and after trying to squeeze into an extra pair of Nancy's rubber boots, I remembered my granny boots in Bumpa's closet. They were still there. The sheets had been stripped from Bumpa's bed, but other than that, everything looked the same. I sat down on the bed and laced up my boots. Several of the hooks were broken and I had to knot one of the ties. I thought of the riderless horse at JFK's funeral, with the boots turned backward in the stirrups. My "first love" boots had now become my funeral boots.

The blizzard kept most people away from the wake, so we had a lot of time to spend with Bumpa in his open coffin. Nancy poked him to make sure he wasn't playing a trick on us. "Nancy, you stop that!" my mother said. Nancy sat back down in one of the many empty chairs lining the room.

At the funeral mass, the priest kept calling Bumpa by the wrong name, extolling his brave combat service when he'd been a merchant marine on a luxury liner. "This is ridiculous," I whispered to my mother, who quickly hushed me up. The undertakers hadn't been sure if they'd be able to dig a hole in the frozen ground, and we didn't know until the last moment if the burial would take place. After the funeral, we finally got the go-ahead and drove to the cemetery, which was located across train tracks, adjacent to a gravel pit and bus depot. In my granny boots, I trudged up the hill to where Bumpa was buried next to his wife. My mother was too distraught to comfort us. She'd gotten into an argument with her father the morning he died and blamed herself for his death.

"He was too young," she said.

"He was eighty-six," I reminded her. "It was his time." But she insisted it was the wrong time and that she could have saved him, and since he was her father and not mine, I couldn't possibly understand.

"Did they at least take him out feetfirst? That's what he always said he wanted."

"I have no idea! How could you even think of such a thing?"

On Christmas, I opened the present Bumpa had wrapped several days earlier. It was a Japanese woodcut of two tiny figures in a snowstorm that had belonged to my grandmother, who had once lived in Yokohama. He'd had it framed especially for me.

I took the woodcut upstairs to Bumpa's bedroom and cried harder than I'd ever cried in my life. His foot roller and a half-empty bottle of liniment were still on the floor of the closet, next to his Converse walking shoes. Before I returned to New York, I said good-bye to my granny boots and dumped them in the trash. Now they were buried too.

༄

Scott and I moved out of our cold-water flat into a one-bedroom on the corner of Bleecker and 10th streets. He composed songs on his upright piano, while I wrote the lyrics. I fantasized that we'd become a famous songwriting team, like Burt Bacharach and Carole Bayer Sager. When we weren't going to jazz clubs, we'd have dinner with his father and stepmother at dimly lit Third Avenue restaurants with great hamburgers and lots of red wine.

One afternoon in midsummer, we were invited to see their new country home in Dutchess County. A classic white colonial on Quaker Hill, it was across the way from where the globe-trotting journalist Lowell Thomas lived. Thomas had traveled with T. E. Lawrence during World War I and had helped create the legend of Lawrence of Arabia.

Scott's stepmother had collaborated with her decorator to make the house look artfully quaint, as if generations of one family had lived there and had passed down their prized heirlooms. Though the house was deeded with "lake rights," the lake commission, in a move Scott's father attributed to anti-Semitism, rescinded them, and he threatened to file a complaint with the state's Human Rights Commission. In all the years I'd known Scott, I'd never heard anyone mention Judaism, and his father's second wife was a Presbyterian. Nevertheless, Scott's father expected us to go to the lake to "take a stand." As someone who'd spent her summers at the seashore, I hated lakes, particularly ones in disputed waters.

"I think I'm just going to stay behind," I told Scott.

"You can't," he said. "My father wants everybody there."

We all piled into the car, including Scott's nine-year-old stepsister, who was blond and looked just like her mother. Reaching the lake, we put down our blanket on the gravelly sand, while the other families gave us the WASP cold shoulder. Nobody smiled, waved, or even acknowledged our existence. Finally, Scott's father announced, "Let's go swimming!" Everybody turned around, and I imagined them saying, "Here come the Jews!" Technically, there were only two Jews, but I immediately felt guilty making that distinction. "Isn't this great?" Scott's father said as we mimed having fun. I fantasized that Scott, with his lifesaving certificate, would rescue a little platinum-haired kid, and the family would be so grateful they'd cede the lake rights. But we were the only ones in the water because it wasn't even 70 degrees outside. There were people on the beach wearing Fair Isle sweaters. When the modest sun slipped behind the trees and I had goose bumps the size of eggs, we finally walked out of the lake, picked up the blanket, and drove back to the house.

"Why would your father want to go to a lake where he wasn't

wanted?" I asked Scott on the way home. He shrugged and turned up the car radio. As usual, his mother had the most succinct answer: "Because the stupid shithead bastard wants to be a WASP."

⚘

The publishing company didn't have a full-time job for me, and I didn't want to continue fact-checking travel information, so Scott's father hired me freelance to write a guidebook for guests staying in high-end hotels. I was hardly an expert in the luxury sector. I'd stayed in only two semi-nice hotels, courtesy of Scott's father, who'd made the arrangements through a travel publisher. The gay nudist hotel wasn't his fault. The publisher had sent us to report on a Windjammer Cruise around the Caribbean, but the clipper ship sprang a leak and we wound up at a new resort on the French side of St. Martin.

"Don't you think it's weird that everybody's naked?" I asked, looking around.

"You're such a prude," he said.

"But they're all men."

"Maybe the women are indoors."

"This isn't Saudi Arabia! We're on a French island. The French are famous for going topless. The only person's who's topless is a man, and he's wearing a nipple ring."

Scott stripped off his bathing suit and went into the water. I sat on the beach pretending to read. A man walked over to say hello, his uncircumcised, semi-erect penis exactly at eye level.

"Is that your brother?" he asked, pointing to Scott.

I was tempted to say, *Oh, yes, my brother and I travel to nudist resorts all over the world so I can help him pick up men. It's just like* Suddenly, Last Summer, *and he's Monty Clift and I'm Elizabeth Taylor.*

After that vacation, I told Scott I wasn't going anywhere if it involved lakes or gay nudist hotels. Unfortunately, I didn't have the presence of mind to exclude resorts that attracted swinging singles. When the travel publisher asked if we wanted to check out a new hotel in Ocho Rios, Jamaica, we figured why not. While Scott went off to listen to reggae music, where he met one of the many local ganja dealers, I sat by the pool and read Renata Adler's *Speedboat*. Perhaps because it had "speed" in the title, a middle-aged man with a large stomach waddled over from his lounge chair and said, "I assume you like to swing. My girlfriend's a pretty lady. We could have a threesome."

"I've got a boyfriend."

"Then a foursome."

"No, thank you."

"Then what are you doing here?"

"Ask him," I said, pointing to Scott, who'd gotten high and was wearing a stupid grin.

"Up for a little hanky-panky?" the man said, waving to his significant other. She hoisted herself out of the pool and walked over. She was wearing a bikini with a silver chain connecting the top and bottom, and she had a tattoo of a dagger jutting out from her pubic region.

We spent the rest of the vacation avoiding them. I was so desperate I even agreed to go water rafting with the ganja dealer, who, as it turned out, was a classically trained musician. He wanted to know if we had any connections at Juilliard.

"This is the last time I'm going on one of your father's stupid vacations," I told Scott on the way to the airport.

The Kingston airport was jammed with tourists carrying oversize straw baskets and security guards in mirrored aviator sunglasses looking for drug smugglers. As the country's primary crop, marijuana was routinely brought into the United States, and Scott, with his long curly hair, looked like a prime suspect. I hoped he hadn't been dumb enough to stick a few joints in his suitcase. Was it my imagination or did he smell of pot? Right then, I saw myself spending the rest of my life in a Jamaican prison cell.

The swinger and his partner were on our flight, carrying several wooden masks and a fertility statue. He was wearing a Bob Marley T-shirt, she a crocheted mini. They smelled of sweat and patchouli. "Hello!" They waved, walking right over to us. "Did you have fun?" The man winked.

A guard motioned us over to a long table, where several customs officials rifled through everybody's bags. If they caught Scott with anything, I'd pretend I was traveling with the swingers, who were now French-kissing. I'd explain that I was doing a magazine article on "What to Pack for a Swinging Vacation." I wouldn't even need to go into much detail, because the guards were already dumping the contents of their suitcases on the table. Out spilled a whip, several dildos, a tube of lubricant, black pasties, and a few other things I couldn't identify. Convinced one of the dildos contained drugs, the official kept twisting it, until it made a loud vibrating noise. As for the bright pink strap-on, which came with a black leather harness, the officials were so fascinated, they waved us through without checking a thing.

ॐ

The trip to Jamaica was the last vacation we took together. We'd fallen out of love, or at least I had, and I suspected he had too. He was spending more time with his musician friends, coming home late at night, and while I always wanted to talk, no matter the hour, he seemed annoyed that he couldn't sneak in unobserved. Years later, it dawned on me that he might have been seeing someone else, but I never had any proof. I did know one thing: I was stagnating in both my career and my relationship, but I couldn't imagine breaking up. Falling back on an old acting exercise, I'd walk across Bleecker Street, down Christopher, and try to "feel" what it was like to leave. It felt scary. Where would I live? Who would hire me? How would I pay my rent? Complicating matters was that while I was no longer in love with Scott, I still loved him and that affection ran deep. What if I never saw him again?

I was turning twenty-six that January and decided to use that milestone as my deadline to leave. I bought a pair of T-strap heels as an early birthday present, hoping I'd wear them on exciting job interviews or dates. I was getting myself totally psyched. Of course I planned to leave after my birthday because I couldn't imagine spending it alone.

The night before my birthday, we had dinner with his father and stepmother at a French restaurant on the Upper East Side. The waiter recommended steak tartare, and not realizing it was raw meat, I ordered it. When it arrived, I thought I was going to be sick, but not wanting to appear unsophisticated, I picked at it, while drinking too much red wine on an empty stomach.

After dinner, Scott dropped me off at the apartment while he went to park the car. Feeling tipsy, I took off my new shoes and ran into the bathroom, slamming my right foot against the door. The pain was excruciating. I looked down at my little toe, which now reared off at a grotesque right angle. I'd remembered reading that a broken toe had to be secured to its "brother," but all I could find was thick silver automotive tape. I wrapped the toe and kept on going. When Scott returned, he found me writhing on the floor, my entire leg wrapped in silver.

"What the hell happened?" he asked. "Did you break your leg?"

"No, my little toe."

Scott took me to St. Vincent's Hospital, which has since closed but was then on Greenwich Avenue. It was after midnight, and the emergency room was filled with the types of people who tend to get into trouble when everyone else is asleep. Some had been stabbed, others shot, a few had OD'd, and one had a tire stuck on his head. Even with my mysterious silver leggings, I was a very low priority. At six A.M., Scott left to get a few hours of sleep before heading off to work.

Two hours later, I was finally brought into an examining room. "Hey, I bet you didn't expect to be celebrating your birthday in a hospital," the young doctor said. He looked at the automotive tape. "Were you out partying or something?"

"I broke my toe on the bathroom door."

"I guess you got carried away with the tape," he said as he ripped it off. "Wow, that's a bad break. I don't think I've ever seen such a weird configuration."

"Don't I need X-rays? Maybe we should consult a foot surgeon?"

"No, I just need to reset it."

He pulled out a pencil from a drawer. I figured he was going to take notes, so I began to explain how it happened, but he said, "Shhh . . . close your eyes." Placing the toe over the pencil, he re-broke it, while I hollered in pain.

"Are you crazy?" I yelled. "Are you even a doctor?"

"Intern," he said. "I learned the pencil trick in med school, but this is the first time I ever got to do it. That was cool." He taped the little toe to its "brother" and told me to come back in a month.

When I returned for my checkup, he removed the tape, and my little toe was still sticking out at the same right angle. "Oh, this isn't good," he said. Before I could yell, "*No, not the pencil!*" he whipped it out and broke the toe again.

It was such a bad break I was on crutches off and on for a month. That put a crimp in my plans to leave. I wrote a short story about my experience in the hospital, which I read to Scott. "I don't like your writing," he said. "You're not very funny."

Despite my encouragement, he was giving up his dream of becoming a musician in favor of going into the business side of music. His father thought it was more practical, and Scott was now talking about opening a recording studio. "You're a wonderful musician," I said. "Don't listen to your father."

The next day, Scott's father informed me that I no longer had a job. "People are talking too much about the affair," he explained.

"I'd hardly call it an affair. We've been together since college."

"No, the affair with me."

"But I'm not having an affair with you."

"That's what people are saying."

I didn't even know how to respond. Scott's father, who was twice my age, was practically a newlywed. Did he have such a reputation as a stud that it seemed plausible that he'd cheat on his young wife with his son's even younger girlfriend?

When Scott came home, I told him that his father had fired me because everybody thought we were having an affair.

"Really?"

"Apparently so." The situation was so ridiculous I started to laugh and couldn't stop. Tears streamed down my face. "Why would I have an affair with your father?" I said, barely able to get out the words. "He . . . doesn't . . . even . . . have . . . lake rights."

"That's not the slightest bit funny. My father is planning to bring the lake committee before the Human Rights Commission."

"Maybe I should sue your father for sex discrimination." At that point, I was practically rolling on the floor, and Scott, disgusted, went into the other room to read his favorite new book—*Star-Making Machinery: Inside the Business of Rock and Roll.*

A month later, I moved into a small apartment on the Upper West Side and began my new job as an editor of a travel newsletter. I wasn't crazy about the apartment, and I didn't like the job, but at least I'd cut my ties to Scott.

10

The Oxford Boys

I've always loved oxfords, and as I write this, they're back in fashion again. Victoria Beckham, of the sky-high stilettos and bountiful Birkins, not only showed them in her most recent collection but was also photographed wearing them. This is very good news for the classic tie shoe that derived from the Oxonian, a style of half-boot that was popular at Oxford University. For years it was associated mainly with college men, lesbians, librarians, and Salvation Army ladies.

I bought my first pair in 1977, after I saw Diane Keaton in *Annie Hall*. The movie won the Oscar for Best Picture and set off a major trend for menswear on women. While I didn't adopt the ties or goofy hats, I loved the white shirt buttoned to the neck, the baggy khakis, tweed jacket, and, of course, the oxfords. The shoes elicited interesting reactions from men. "Very few women can pull those off," said a fellow writer, without adding, "But you can." Another man called me a dyke on the subway, which made me wonder what was so threatening to men about women co-opting their accessories. Did they think that once women wore oxfords, they'd march into a man's office, step on his toes, kick him in the balls, and plant their two sturdy feet on his desk?

Luckily, I found two men who loved oxfords and, in different ways, loved me. The first I met through my film school friend, who dragged me to a dinner party on the Upper West Side. Woody was a screenwriter and journalist who kept a sprawling film archive in his Riverside Drive apartment. In addition to 5,000 videotapes that were cataloged alphabetically, the place was totally filled with stacks of newspapers and magazines waiting to be clipped and filed. People who saw the apartment never forgot it, often comparing Woody to the Collyer brothers, the famous Harlem hoarders who lived and died neck-deep in rubble. Woody was an ebullient host. Though three inches shorter than I, with oversize glasses and wispy auburn hair, he had a rich baritone voice and sexy, self-confident manner. Tunneling my way through pillars of print, I sat down on a bunch of old *Time* magazines, while Woody poured wonton soup into mugs. His father had been the chief theoretician of the American Socialist Party, so he was careful to apportion the wontons equally, but when he reached me, he dropped two extra into my mug. I knew I'd be hearing from him.

Woody loved being a mentor, and I badly needed one. The only traveling I did as a travel writer was to the company's headquarters in suburban Bronxville. On our first date, Woody told me I was wasting my talent. On our second date, I came down with the flu and he brought me chicken soup. On our third date, he invited me to Europe. On our sixth date, we went to JFK.

Woody had managed to rack up an impressive array of magazine assignments that took us to Paris and London. As might be expected of a man who lived in an archive, he did not travel light, lugging forty-three file boxes of research material with him. After we'd loaded everything into a van he'd rented at the Paris airport, we moved into a two-bedroom apartment in the Marais. It belonged to an old friend whose heiress niece had left an Elsa Peretti diamonds-by-the-yard necklace dangling from the pull cord to the toilet. Vedic cosmology charts were taped to an entire wall. There was no refrigerator, so we ate our dinners in neighborhood bistros. Woody was a great mimic, with an incredible ear for accents. Though he knew only a few French phrases, he spoke them like a native.

Waiters were totally confused when after he'd order *"steak au poivre, bleu, s'il vous plaît,"* they'd ask a question and he'd respond, *"Je ne comprend pas,"* in perfect-sounding French. Once a taxicab driver talked to him for fifteen minutes after he'd pronounced our street address with such Gallic verve that the driver didn't seem to notice that the rest of Woody's conversation consisted of *"Oui"* and *"Bien-sûr."*

One of Woody's assignments was to interview the great film composer Georges Delerue, who had recently composed the soundtrack for George Cukor's *Rich and Famous*. Delerue had scored many of Truffaut's films, including my favorite—*Jules and Jim*—about a love triangle between two men and a woman, and I was eager to meet him. We had lunch at one of Delerue's favorite restaurants, where everyone assumed Woody spoke the language. At that point I think even Woody thought he spoke it. The movie publicist eventually straightened things out and Woody conducted the interview through a translator, but not before receiving multiple compliments on his "beautiful French."

In London, I interviewed most of the cast members of *The Rocky Horror Picture Show* for the "official poster magazine." Woody had helped me get the assignment. It wasn't what I'd gone to film school for, but as Woody reminded me, in his Humphrey Bogart accent, I needed "the dough." Since I hadn't seen the *Rocky Horror* play or the movie I was somewhat at a disadvantage, but after Woody pointed me to the right boxes, I could have performed a one-woman show of it.

With a brief stop in New York to pick up more boxes, Woody and I drove to Tucson, where he'd been assigned to write a story about *The Villain*. Directed by former stuntman Hal Needham, it starred Kirk Douglas, Ann-Margret, and, in his first romantic lead, the former bodybuilder and future governor of California, Arnold Schwarzenegger. The movie was a broad comedy caper based on the Road Runner cartoons, and they'd built an old Western town complete with saloon and "pleasure house" in nearby Rio Rico.

Feeling like a city slicker in my oxfords, I told Woody we needed Western boots.

"I'm Annie Hall when I should be Annie Oakley," I explained. Woody was a huge fan of Westerns—he'd seen John Ford's *The Searchers* at least thirty times—but there was no way he was going to wear cowboy boots. He favored L. L. Bean boat shoes, which he wore everywhere, except on boats. He agreed to drive me to Tucson, where I saw boots in every available color and skin, from ostrich to armadillo. The salesman, who was weighted down in turquoise and silver, asked what I wanted. "Something subtle," I said. He looked crushed, so I added "but with texture." He suggested Lucchese. The only Lucchese I knew had been head of a New York crime family and bore the nickname Three Finger, but apparently he was from a different branch. The Texas Luccheses had established the boot company in 1883, outfitting the U.S. Cavalry. The salesman explained that Lucchese had boots unique to every state, complete with depictions of the state flag, flower, and bird.

"What state are you from?" he asked.

"Massachusetts."

"I'm not sure we have that boot. Where do you live now?"

"New York."

"I don't think we have that one either."

He wondered if perhaps I might like the Montana boot, which was one of his favorites. I told him that if I were going to buy a "state boot," I'd probably want to have visited the state at least once.

"If you really like them, we could go," Woody said. His mix of sweetness and total impracticality was a source of constant amazement to me.

I settled on a stateless boot, in brown lizard skin, with hand-tooled curlicues running down the sides. I tried to scuff them up to make them look as if I'd had them for more than five minutes, but they still screamed *city slicker*.

Woody's first interview was with Hal Needham, who was on a career high after directing *Smokey and the Bandit*, starring his best friend, Burt Reynolds. Prior to directing, Needham had enjoyed a stellar career as a stuntman, wrecking cars, leaping from horses, and breaking fifty-six bones and his back twice.

"I think we're going to be pals," Woody said.

Woody assumed that doing an interview was the start of a beautiful friendship, when it was usually only the start of a professional relationship that ended once the story hit the newsstand.

"I don't think you're going to become 'pals' with a daredevil stunt driver," I said. "You have nothing in common."

Woody put on his hurt face. "Yes, we do. We both love movies."

Though *The Villain* was supposed to be a comedy, the only thing I found amusing was the sight of Schwarzenegger strolling around in a powder-blue cowboy suit that barely contained his bulging muscles.

During a lunch break, I helped myself to some rice and beans from the craft service table, taking refuge in our rental car. Suddenly, the door opened and Schwarzenegger, minus the ten-gallon hat but still in the powder-blue cowboy ensemble, squeezed behind the steering wheel. The seat had been adjusted to Woody's height and Schwarzenegger was practically curled into a ball. Dispensing with the niceties, he got straight to the point: *"Doomp the leetle guy and be vid me."*

I was so startled, I dumped the beans and rice all over my lap. Schwarzenegger didn't seem to notice. *"Vat* you doing *vid* him anyway?" he wanted to know.

Schwarzenegger was so huge it was like sitting in the front row at a drive-in movie. I'd never seen such a large head or hands. As he attempted to extricate himself from the car, he said, "We'll *cadge up layder."*

From then on, I couldn't make a move without Schwarzenegger following me. Realizing the he-man approach hadn't worked, he tried the courtly method.

"I can tell you *ah* a woman who likes *ahht."*

"I'm sorry, I like what?"

"Ahhhht! Ahhht!"

"Oh, art. Yes, I like it."

"Then we *chute* go to a museum together. There *ah* many *intresting* ones around."

"We're in the middle of the desert. Where are the museums?"

He didn't know exactly but said we could go to any number of them and then have dinner.

"I don't think that's a good idea."

"You don't?" He looked crestfallen, as if he couldn't believe somebody wouldn't want to go to a nonexistent museum in a partially fake desert with a muscleman in a powder-blue lace-up shirt.

"I like your boots," he persisted. "Where did you get them?"

I couldn't remember the name of the shop, and anyway I didn't want to go boot shopping with him. Next he offered to buy me a pair.

"No, thanks. I already have these."

He shook his head, and then, putting on his ten-gallon hat, he lumbered toward the Pleasure House.

⁂

After Tucson, we drove to L.A., where Woody interviewed George Cukor about *Rich and Famous,* which starred Jacqueline Bisset and Candice Bergen. Cukor, who was then eighty, had worked in Hollywood for sixty years, with such major stars as Greta Garbo, Ingrid Bergman, Audrey Hepburn, and Marilyn Monroe. Cukor's greatest collaboration, however, was with Katharine Hepburn, whom he directed in eight films, including *Holiday* and *The Philadelphia Story.* I'd always loved Hepburn, whose mannish style was a forerunner to Diane Keaton's, and whose affection for oxfords placed her in the company of such sexually ambiguous stars as Greta Garbo and Marlene Dietrich. All three adopted the shoe for its comfort and subversive chic. Hepburn often paired them with loose-fitting trousers known as Oxford Bags, named after a popular style of slouchy pants that Oxford students favored.

In homage to Hepburn, I wore my version of Oxford Bags, along with my oxford shoes. Greeting us at the door of his home in the Hollywood Hills, Cukor, looking at Woody and then at me, said, "Well, *she's* much prettier than you are."

I was floating on air. The man who'd directed Garbo and Hepburn had called *me* pretty. Maybe he'd cast me in his next movie; though, given his advanced age, he'd have to work pretty fast.

Cukor took us on a tour of his house, a Mediterranean-style villa that Billy Haines, the actor-turned-designer, had decorated in the mid-1930s. We walked down a hallway filled with autographed photos of his movie star friends, into a library lined with autographed books by F. Scott Fitzgerald, Somerset Maugham, and Thomas Mann. "I think we're going to be pals," Woody whispered. Settling into the living room, he pulled out his tape recorder and began the interview. I knew from all the boxes marked *Cukor* that Woody had spent a lot of time on research. He started as he always did, at the beginning, which in this case was 1930. Cukor was initially flattered with Woody's encyclopedic knowledge of his career, but after two hours, Cukor stood up and said, "I've had enough." Woody couldn't believe it. "But we haven't even gotten to *Rich and Famous,*" he said. Cukor didn't care. "You're a very selfish young man taking up so much of my time. Now get out."

I ran out of the house while Woody collected his things. A few minutes later, we were standing on the lawn when Cukor opened the door. "Feel free to take a swim," he said breezily. The pool looked exactly like the one in *The Philadelphia Story*. Hepburn and Tracy had lived in two cottages on the property.

"We don't have bathing suits," Woody said.

"You can go skinny dipping," Cukor replied.

"Should we?" Woody asked.

All I could picture was the opening scene in *Sunset Boulevard* with the corpse of the screenwriter Joe Gillis floating in Norma Desmond's pool. "You're crazy," I told him. "Cukor might kill you." We started to laugh and couldn't stop. We were still laughing as we climbed into our rental car and drove back to our Sherman Oaks rental apartment.

Several days later, Woody introduced me to his best friend, Warren, who lived in a magical 1930s Hollywood bungalow partially hidden in a maze of bougainvillea. Warren could have easily stepped out of an old movie; he was tall and handsome, with enough family money to allow him to indulge his various hobbies, which included collecting vintage movie posters. When I noticed *Holiday* and *The Philadelphia Story* mounted prominently on the wall, I told him my Cukor story, which by then had taken on a life of its own.

"Yes, I can see why he thought you looked like Katharine Hepburn," he said.

"Oh, it was probably just the oxfords," I replied modestly.

Warren had a separate photography studio on his property, where he took pictures of rock singers and aspiring actresses. He asked if he could do a shoot with me, and I agreed, although my previous experience with photographers had not been overly positive. My father's picture-taking efforts frequently ended in tears because my mother usually had something critical to say. Scott conveniently lost all our photographs after we split up. Warren's pictures of me exuded a 1930s glamour that was all the more remarkable because I hated being in front of a camera. Warren had a great eye. He also had a motivation problem, which didn't bode well for a sustained photography career, but at heart, he was a true collector, not only of movie posters but vintage photographs and postcards and anything that evoked the romantic past.

Woody and Warren had known each other in high school, cementing their friendship as film students at NYU. The two had a "bromance" long before the term existed. Not only did they share a love of movies and collecting, but they were also hysterically funny, each trying to outdo the other. Often they'd laugh so hard that tears would run down Woody's cheeks. It was hard not to feel like a third wheel. Woody got along better with Warren than he did with me. They were "pals" in the truest sense.

After nine months of being on the road, Woody and I finally settled back in New York, where we cemented our relationship with a wire fox terrier named Katie. Eager to avoid any behavior issues, Woody immediately hired the "Dog Commander." With her porcelain skin and cascading curls, the Commander looked as if she'd come straight from a Renaissance fair, but behind the Pre-Raphaelite exterior lurked a canine dominatrix. Snapping Katie's leash like a whip, she barked orders in a cool, firm voice. Terriers, she cautioned, have a stubborn streak, and it was important to establish who was boss. To help regulate the dog's schedule, we had to make sure she ate her meals at a set time every day. The minute she finished, one of us had to take her outside. Beginning at seven P.M., we had to withhold water so she wouldn't need to urinate in the middle of the night. During the day, the Commander ordered us to keep a sharp eye on her to avoid any accidents. The best way to do that, she explained, was to attach a long lead to her collar and then place it around one of our ankles.

Woody posted a weekly "Dog Schedule" in the kitchen, specifying who would walk the dog and when; who would keep the dog fastened to his or her leg; and who would practice the Dog Commander's lessons. Woody believed in an equal division of labor, which was perfectly fair, but I began to view him as the Human Commander.

Meanwhile, Warren sublet an apartment for six months in Woody's building. While Woody cooked his signature dish—Spaghetti Woody—Warren would discuss his love life with me. He had been in therapy for years and was the epitome of the new cultural icon: the "sensitive man." Yet he was totally unrealistic when it came to women, expecting them to live up to a movie star ideal, but since no woman could compare to the celluloid Katharine Hepburn or his other favorite star, the helmet-haired Louise Brooks, he was always disappointed. It kept him safe from having to commit to a relationship, as did his unfortunate habit of becoming infatuated with his friends' girlfriends. After I once told him that he looked better without his glasses, he'd whip them off whenever we got together, and then bat his blue eyes.

One night, as we were all sitting on Woody's bed eating Spaghetti Woody and watching Katharine Hepburn in *The Philadelphia Story* for the umpteenth time, I began to weigh the pros and cons of both men. Woody was a hard worker. Warren didn't like to work. Woody had to watch his money. Warren watched it fly out the window. Woody was short. Warren was tall. Woody lived in the real world. Warren lived in a fantasy. My polygamous fantasy ended, however, when Warren returned to L.A. and fell in love with a singer/songwriter who fulfilled his twin fantasies: She looked like Louise Brooks *and* she'd been involved with one of his friends.

After a lavish wedding at Tavern on the Green, the newly married couple moved from L.A. to New York, where Warren opened a movie poster gallery. The gallery's logo was based on his favorite poster: a spectacular life-size one-sheet of a sultry Louise Brooks in G. W. Pabst's *Diary of a Lost Girl*. As for the real Louise, she was a total free spirit who found herself caught up in a whirl of mandatory parties. Warren's extended family was a large one, and now that the "prodigal son" had returned, he was expected to attend all the black-tie bar mitzvahs and other events he'd moved to L.A. to avoid. With her aspiring singing career in limbo, Louise was truly a lost girl; she spent her days getting facials and buying shoes. I wasn't envious of the family parties, but as a struggling writer, I was definitely envious of the shoes.

༼ༀ༽

By the early 1980s, oxfords had fallen out of fashion in favor of "look-at-me" footwear. The Reagan presidency, with tax policies that favored the upper class, resulted in a period of conspicuous consumption not seen since the Gilded Age. Nothing was considered too over-the-top, from Lacroix $15,000 "pouf" dresses, to financier Saul Steinberg's fiftieth birthday party, featuring actors posing as re-creations of famous Old Masters paintings. Money was increasingly fracturing Manhattan, with artists being driven from SoHo lofts to make room for investment bankers who wanted to live like artists.

Women's shoes exemplified the growing class divide. The 1980 New York City transit strike prompted thousands of female employees to don sneakers. For a "working girl," like Melanie Griffith in the Mike Nichols movie of the same name, the trend continued after the strike because they couldn't afford to take taxis, and sneakers were more comfortable when dealing with subways, buses, and ferries. Women who didn't need or want to work could indulge in fantasy shoes that mirrored their rarefied lifestyles.

The designer Maud Frizon best captured the era's over-the-top frivolity. With their eye-popping metallic colors, scalloped edges, and butterfly appliqués, Frizon's shoes had a rock star/fairy princess quality that appealed to the imagination. Her personal story was equally seductive. A former Parisian model, she'd married an Italian shoe salesman who'd fallen in love with her "perfect" size 6 feet. With their two children, they lived in a chateau in the Loire Valley, where she dreamed up fanciful shoe designs while he handled the business. When I later described Frizon's enviable life to my therapist, she said, "Ah! The 'unseen hands'!" She was referring to Jean Cocteau's film *Beauty and the Beast*, in which invisible hands catered to Beauty's every need. Frizon's whimsical creations, with their astronomical price tags, symbolized a life where I could write without intrusions—a room of one's own, with invisible servants, and a massive shoe closet.

I was then working in a small back room in Woody's apartment, where I had to climb a Matterhorn of periodicals to reach my desk. Living in a pseudo library should have been conducive to writing, but it wasn't. Woody could toss off a story in a matter of hours, while I'd labor over each sentence. Though I wanted to be equally productive, I constantly fell short, and Woody would then lecture me on developing better organizational skills. I realized I needed a place of my own. I'd loved his back room for the comfort it gave me, just as I loved Spaghetti Woody and regular Woody. I adored his brilliant mind, vast knowledge of history, wonderful sense of humor, and huge heart. He was totally unique, and I knew I'd never find anyone quite like him. And then there was Warren, who had recently purchased the actor William Powell's 1930s velvet smoking jacket; he was trying to remake himself and Louise into the urbane husband-and-wife team, played by Powell and Myrna Loy, in the *Thin Man* movies. If Woody and I split up, who'd gain custody of Warren?

Woody and I had always had a fairly combustible relationship, but as I'd outgrown my protégé role and he'd grown tired of mentoring me, we began to bicker over stupid things—who'd walk the dog, do the dishes, buy the spaghetti. I wanted to move back into my old apartment, but Emily, who'd followed me to New York, was living in it. She'd become a talented jewelry designer but wasn't making a lot of money and I felt responsible for her. As a result, I didn't want to evict her from my Upper West Side apartment and she didn't want to leave. This caused a lot of tension between us and prolonged my deteriorating relationship with Woody.

The tipping point finally happened when I accidentally caused Woody's dishwasher to overflow, flooding the kitchen. He claimed I nearly drowned the dog. That night, I left his apartment and moved in with Emily. I immediately called Warren to tell him, but he was on the phone with Woody. I wanted to call Woody, but I'd just broken up with him.

This was during the Christmas season, which is a terrible time to break up with someone. Before heading to Andover for the holidays, I went to Macy's to buy presents for everyone. I'd always been careful never to carry large sums of money, but I had $700 in cash for the presents and to repay Woody for groceries and supplies, including $300 worth of toilet paper. Apparently, I was unduly extravagant with it. While dawdling in the shoe department, someone stole my pocketbook, and I lost the money, my credits cards, and my license. It was all too much. I called Warren and cried into the pay phone. A few hours later, he showed up at my apartment with $700 in cash. "I've always wanted to be a knight in shining armor," he said sweetly.

In January, Woody asked me to come over to pack up the rest of my things. It was my thirtieth birthday, and I'd spent the day cleaning the apartment and suggesting to Emily that she might want to contact a real estate agent. I walked over to Woody's dressed in dirty sweat clothes, with unwashed hair and no makeup. When I opened the door, I heard "Surprise!" Woody had planned a birthday party for me before we'd split up. He didn't think it was honorable to cancel.

"This is totally embarrassing," I said when I got him alone. "What could you have been thinking?"

"You told me you'd always wanted a surprise birthday party."

"But we've split up."

"So?" he said.

"Which means we're no longer together."

"Yes, we are," he said. "It's just that now we're pals."

I looked at his sweet face, rumpled plaid shirt, and innocent smile. For once, I couldn't argue with him. We were—and there was no better word for it—"pals."

Six months after their wedding, Warren and Louise threw a party, where Warren announced they were planning to buy a country house. Louise was standing next to him as if he'd just announced a run for the presidency, and like many a political spouse, she didn't seem overjoyed. But unlike many a political spouse, she was also wearing a fabulous pair of Maud Frizons. Louise had an elusive quality, which along with her beautiful face, was a great part of her appeal to Warren. Once, when I interviewed her for a magazine article, she confided that she'd lived as a mistress to a famous Western artist and had ended her brief marriage by jumping overboard during a sailing trip.

"Did you know that Louise ended her first marriage by jumping overboard?" I mentioned to Warren, who'd forgotten that Louise had been married. "Doesn't that concern you just a little?"

It didn't. Warren was so totally besotted that when Louise expressed a desire to move back to L.A. to pursue her singing career, he rented a house for her on the aptly named Wonderland Avenue. "I don't think she's going to come back," I told Woody, who accused me of being overly cynical. "Of course, she is," he said. "She's a pal."

After two years of marriage, Louise essentially jumped overboard again, leaving Warren and her Maud Frizon shoes behind. Technically, it was Warren who called it quits; he didn't want an aspiring rock singer as a wife, especially one who was living on Wonderland Avenue when he was on West 66th Street. With Woody at his side, Warren flew to the Dominican Republic to get a quickie divorce.

They played poker on the plane. Woody, a brilliant card player, for once let Warren win. Later, I helped Warren pack up Louise's belongings. When he went into another room to answer the phone, I tried on a pair of her Maud Frizons. I wish I could report that they fit perfectly and that out of the ruins of Warren's marriage, I inherited a fabulous shoe collection. But that only happens in fairy tales.

11

The Blahnik-Puma Wedding

After Woody and I split up, I went on a number of blind dates, mainly with neurologists who had already been married and divorced several times. I don't remember how I got on the neurology dating circuit. I'm as interested in the human brain as anyone, but I'm also smart enough to know that someone who's been divorced multiple times is not necessarily great husband material. When a friend fixed me up with an art curator, I was happy to move on to something different. The curator had never been married and by the end of our lunch date I realized why. He told me I looked exactly like "a Modigliani" and then went on to explain that the model was the artist's mistress—Jeanne Hébuterne, who'd jumped out a window, killing herself and her unborn child.

"You really should have stopped at the 'You look like a Modigliani' part," I said.

"Why? I think it's very romantic," he said. "She killed herself a day after he died. Her headstone reads, 'Devoted companion to the extreme sacrifice.'"

"Check, please."

By the time Warren asked if I wanted to go on a date with an old friend from his high school football team, I was skeptical.

"What does he do?" I wanted to know.

"Finance," Warren said.

"What kind?" Warren wasn't sure. He was incredibly obtuse when it came to business because he rarely had to think about it.

He and the high school football player, whose name was Lee, had recently run into each other at a wedding, where they began reminiscing about Warren's star turn as the lead singer of their school's rock group. Apparently, he'd garnered legions of teenage groupies who treated him like a god. Having missed Warren's traumatic descent from Mount Olympus, Lee still thought of him as the Deity of Dating and figured he'd have a little black book chock-full of names. The only suitable name was mine.

"I'm feeling a little guilty," Warren confessed.

"Why? Because the guy's a loser?"

"No, because I'm being disloyal to Woody."

"That's crazy. Woody and I are getting along better than ever, and he doesn't even mind that I broke up with him."

"He told me he broke up with you."

"Excuse me, but who walked out of the apartment? *Me!*"

"Yeah, but he said he was going to ask you to leave."

"Okay, I'm going on the date."

❧

Lee showed up at my door in a Tyrolean ski sweater and patent-leather Puma sneakers. Who wore patent-leather sneakers? In bright red?

Presuming you'd ever want such hideous things, where would you even find them? Over a Mexican dinner on Columbus Avenue, Lee explained that the sneakers were very rare and could be found only in special stores in Europe. The reason he knew this was that in between college and business school he'd worked for Puma, a German sports company that had previously been Dassler Brothers Shoes. Jesse Owens, the African American sprinter, had worn a pair of their running spikes in the 1936 Berlin Summer Olympics when he won his four gold medals. After a famous feud that divided the small Bavarian town of Herzogenaurach—Lee actually knew how to pronounce it—brothers Rudi and Adi Dassler, who'd been members of the Nazi Party, split up the company.

"Adidas was named for Adi," Lee explained, "and Puma for Rudi."

"Puma sounds nothing like Rudi," I said.

"Maybe he named it after a puma because the cat is so fast."

"Maybe." I was getting a little tired of Adi and Rudi and debated having a second margarita, but since he'd only ordered one beer, I didn't want him to think I was a lush.

"So, what kind of banking do you do?" I asked.

"Technology. Computers, software, things like that."

Except for HAL in *2001: A Space Odyssey,* I'd never given computers a second thought. Who cared about them? Sensing he wasn't scoring big on the technology front, he moved on to sports, explaining that he played tennis, had founded a ski camp with his uncle in the Austrian Alps (hence the Tyrolean sweater), and had been on the football, baseball, and swim teams in high school.

"What did you major in?" I expected him to say "accounting" or "discus throwing" but he surprised me.

"Philosophy."

"Really?"

"Yeah, I like Heraclitus a lot. 'You cannot step twice into the same stream.'"

"Why not?"

"Because everything changes and nothing remains still."

I had a feeling he'd used that line before. After he paid the check, he walked me back to my apartment and a funny thing happened. Despite the red Pumas, we fell neatly into step, as if we'd been walking side by side for decades. Suddenly, I heard a voice whisper, *You will marry this man,* and I thought, *Marry the man? I don't even want to go on another date with him.*

When I got home, I called Warren and said, "He knows nothing about movies and doesn't make me laugh. And he wore red Pumas! If he calls and asks how things went, don't encourage him."

Lee called several days later and invited me to brunch. I agreed because we were destined to marry and my previous plans had fallen through. This time he wore a different Tyrolean sweater, in white, and matching Pumas. At brunch I noticed that he had a dazzling smile, a great head of brown hair, and a freckle beneath one of his dark brown eyes. It was adorable, but a cute freckle couldn't compensate for having nothing in common.

I was then writing full-time for *New York* magazine, and the publicity director, who'd spotted us at brunch, came over to me the next day and asked, "Who was that handsome guy?" I later found out that he reminded her of her husband. So she was slightly biased, but since I thought she was smart and stylish, I decided to invite Lee over to dinner. Also, I'd just completed a cover story, "Mommy Only," about women whose biological clocks were running out and were turning to male friends or sperm banks to have babies. These women were among the early pioneers, and while I admired them for taking control of their lives, I didn't want to be in their shoes.

Though I'd never made anything more complicated than spaghetti and a tuna sandwich, I bought the new *Silver Palate Cookbook* and picked chicken Marbella. Everyone was making it, and if they weren't making it, they were talking about it. It involved prunes and dates and lots of chopping. It also unfortunately involved a chicken, which in its uncooked state was more of an anatomy lesson than I'd bargained for. After getting over my initial revulsion, I marinated it using rubber gloves so I didn't actually have to touch it and then placed it in the refrigerator overnight. The next day we had a blizzard, which made me think of Bumpa's funeral, which of course made me think of Bumpa and his love of cooking. The storm paralyzed the city. The buses and subways weren't running. There were no cabs on the street. Lee, nevertheless, trudged twenty-two blocks to see me. He was wearing special snow boots from Innsbruck and a gigantic insulated coat from Stowe, Vermont, where he'd gone skiing in minus-8-degree weather. Officials were giving them out to people so they wouldn't freeze to death on the chairlift. He'd kept his because you never know when you might need a chairlift coat when it dropped to minus-8 degrees on the subway.

I'd built a fire but had forgotten to open the flue. Lee arrived to find the apartment filled with smoke, the chicken Marbella burnt to a crisp in the oven. He fixed the fire and ate the blackened chicken, which he said was the best he'd ever tasted and this was way before blackened chipotle chicken came into vogue. Could I imagine Woody or Warren trekking through a snowstorm? Would they lie and tell me burnt chicken was delicious? Never! And to make things really perfect, Lee, like Bumpa, loved to cook. I'd never have to make chicken Marbella again, or blackened chipotle chicken. If my luck held out, I'd never again have to touch a chicken.

✺

Lee's friends described him as "very grounded," so imagine my surprise when on our fourth date I found myself 3,000 feet in the air with him. He had just received his glider pilot's license and I was his first passenger. "You must really be desperate for a boyfriend," Nancy said when I told her. It takes a certain amount of trust to sit in the front of a cockpit while someone flies the plane from the backseat. Yes, the sky is beautiful; yes, you're riding thermals with the birds, but your life is in someone else's hands. At first I was terrified, and then after I surrendered control, it became exhilarating and romantic, like the scene in the remake of *The Thomas Crown Affair*. Lee had both feet on the ground while airborne. It was like being with an astronaut.

Afterward, I went back to his Upper West Side apartment, which was decorated in typical straight-guy style: brown and rust color scheme, gigantic modular sofa, huge entertainment unit, and bare dingy walls. While he made dinner, I repaid him for the glorious day by snooping in his bedroom closet. There's really no excuse, but to say that I'd have been happier if I'd found my missing toes pickled in a jar is not an overstatement. There, jammed in with his suits, ties, and, yes, the chairlift coat, were boxes upon boxes of Puma sneakers. He must have had every model ever made, even those dating back to the Nazi era. Though I was trying to be as quiet as I could, you can only open and close so many shoe boxes in a shoe box–size apartment without someone hearing you.

"What are you doing?" Lee asked when he found me in his closet, hiding behind the chairlift coat, sneakers scattered all over the place.

I thought of the scene in *The Great Gatsby*, when Gatsby begins throwing all his shirts around and Daisy, crying, says, "It makes me sad because I've never seen such—such beautiful shirts before."

"It makes me sad because I've never seen so—so many sneakers," I said. And then of course I had to add, "and I think it's very weird."

"Weird is you snooping in my closet," Lee said. "The sneakers are unique and very collectible."

"But they're taking up too much space."

"Why do you care?"

I didn't tell him that if we ever moved in together I'd have no room for my clothes and shoes. Maybe that was his strategy. He was holding on to the Puma sneakers because he was clinging to his single lifestyle. He was commitment phobic. Didn't he tell me on our very first date that pumas are very fast and agile cats? Obviously, the sneakers represented Lee's arrested development and his desire to flee relationships. I also remembered him telling me that one of his favorite TV shows had been *T.H.E. Cat*, which starred Robert Loggia as a retired master jewel thief who worked as a bodyguard out of his friend's café—El Casa del Gato. (Translation: "House of the Cat.") I now feared that Lee, despite our predetermined wedding, would select the perfect Puma sneakers from his vast collection and sprint out of my life faster than Jesse Owens.

❦

Lee stuck around, and two years later, we bought Warren's two-bedroom apartment in Lincoln Center, where Warren had once lived his fairy-tale life with Louise. It wasn't a great apartment, but I had fond memories of Louise's Maud Frizon shoe closet, which, sadly, became Lee's Puma den. Though the sneakers had made the move with us, we gave the rust modular couch to Woody, recently married to a lovely woman who worked in book publishing. They'd eloped to London, gypping us out of a wedding, but we threw them an engagement party in our apartment, which gave people the opportunity to ask, "Hey, didn't Warren used to live here?" and "Doesn't Woody's wife think it's weird you two are still friends?" (For the record, Woody's wife and I ultimately became friends too.)

By now, my parents had given up all hope that I'd ever marry a Catholic, fearing that I'd continue living in sin with a series of men who were going to hell and taking me with them. That aside, they were very fond of Lee. He liked them too, even though the holidays were usually fraught with animal emergencies. Given his fondness for Pumas, it's a shame he missed the Cat Period, which lasted a good decade. Pie, the acrobat, died from complications of an aerial accident but nevertheless lived to a ripe old age. (Nancy attributed it to all the cardio.) Pie's daughter, Pearl, was hit by a car. Pearl's kittens died at the vet's, after my parents dropped off the pregnant cat prior to going on vacation. She refused to nurse them, either because she was traumatized from the move or because she had no maternal instinct, or possibly both. Another cat climbed up a tree and never came down, and yet another jumped out a car window and sprinted down a highway.

Now that my parents were empty nesters, they decided to get a dog, a cairn terrier named McDuff. By the time my mother realized that dogs don't learn discipline through osmosis, McDuff had already begun his fifteen-year Reign of Terror. Bred to ferret out rats and other rodents from piles of rocks, or cairns, he was, in dog lingo, a "ratter." He ruled through a combination of intimidation and chutzpah, setting himself up as the master of the house and laying down certain ground rules, such as "no leash."

Whenever my mother tried to connect a leash to his collar, he'd reveal his vicious side, growling and snapping and threatening to bite her hand. He preferred to be chauffeured around town, sitting in the backseat directly behind my mother. If he was kept waiting in the car too long, she'd pay the price. Once, after a trip to a garden shop, my mother glanced into the rearview mirror to see him baring his teeth like Cujo. He snarled and snapped the whole way home and then wouldn't budge from the backseat. When my father tried to lure him inside, McDuff charged at him, so they let him spend the night in the car, tossing a few dog biscuits and his favorite squeaky toy through the window.

After one particular Thanksgiving, McDuff wound up at the vet's because my mother feared he'd dislocated his neck whipping it around when Lee made the innocent mistake of attempting to connect the leash. He offered to drive the car and in all the confusion he accidentally slammed the door on my mother's finger, so he was two for two.

"I hope McDuff doesn't get all crazy again," he said as we drove to Andover for Easter.

"He will get crazy, because he *is* crazy."

All went well, until my mother, in a brilliant sleight of hand, attached the leash to the dog's collar and took him up the street for a walk. Ten minutes later, she returned, frantic. The big dog in the house on the corner had grabbed McDuff by the throat, drawing blood. McDuff was a little shaken up, but quickly reverted to being his normal psychotic self, growling at the leash hanging on the doorknob. We'd just finished our main course when the doorbell rang. The dog's owner and his little boy wanted to give McDuff an Easter basket full of their dog's toys.

"Our dog won't be bothering you anymore," the father said. "We put him down."

"Excuse me?" I said.

"We put him down," he repeated.

"As in . . . dead?" I asked.

The father nodded.

Apart from finding a vet keen on euthanizing a golden retriever on Easter Sunday, I wondered what kind of father would do such a thing. And the poor kid! Afterward, nobody felt like finishing dinner. My mother was convinced McDuff had sprained his neck again, though you'd never know it by the way he'd dived into the dead dog's Easter basket. He emerged with a rubber toy shaped like a slipper and began chewing it as if it were my mother's finger.

"Maybe we should bring him to New York and let him loose in the Puma closet," I said to Lee.

"My Pumas are precious to me."

"I know."

⁓

We moved again, this time to a larger apartment around the corner from Woody and his wife and their two young children. We had more closet space. We also had the Pumas. Since Lee was traveling so much for work, and I was constantly on deadline, we didn't pay much attention to the next logical step in our relationship: marriage. Whenever one of us brought it up, we usually agreed that we had nothing in common so maybe we should wait until we did.

"We could take up bird-watching when we're in our eighties," I suggested.

"I like birds," he said.

"Yeah, but cats eat them."

"I don't know what you're talking about."

"That's because we have nothing in common."

We could have probably gone on like this for years, except certain things pop up in life to remind us that we don't have as much time as we think we do. My mother developed breast cancer and had a mastectomy, and then I needed a breast biopsy. I had to stay overnight at Memorial Sloan Kettering, and in the morning before the surgery, a nun walked into the room and suggested we pray together. That is when I began to get really nervous. Luckily, the biopsy came back negative, but when my therapist asked why I was waiting so long to get married, I didn't have a good answer.

"Why aren't we married?" I asked Lee one night.

"Because you keep telling me we have nothing in common."

"So what do you want to do?" I pictured him leaping into a pair of Pumas and taking off down Riverside Drive.

"Get married," he said.

✿

Lee wasn't raised in any particular faith—his mother is Italian Catholic, and his father was half-Jewish, half-Episcopalian—so he didn't care who married us. I was wary of choosing a Catholic priest because I couldn't imagine attending the obligatory Pre-Cana classes. Ultimately, a friend recommended a Presbyterian minister who took a more psychological approach to marital counseling.

The minister kicked off our first session with a series of questions beginning with "If you could choose any other profession, what would it be?" I said actress, which wasn't unreasonable, given my theater background. Lee said fashion photographer, which was totally unreasonable, given he'd never even glanced at a fashion magazine and wore a Tyrolean sweater on our first date.

"He thinks Pumas are going to become collectors' items," I explained. "That's how much he knows about fashion."

"What do you have against Pumas?" the minister asked.

"Nothing! I'm just sick of them hogging our closets."

This led to a discussion about how marriage is about sharing and compromise, when I knew it was just about the Pumas. Our final exercise was to fill out a lengthy compatibility test that we flunked. The minister suggested we might want to "rethink" our plans, because it appeared we had nothing in common. By then, it was too late. I'd already gone to Barneys and splurged on a Chanel suit and my first pair of Manolo Blahnik heels. Shoes were now beginning to have names. Soon, you wouldn't be referring to them as "the black thing with the chunky heel" or "the brown flat" but the Manolo D'Orsay, or Manolo Carolyne, or Manolo Campari Mary Jane. I've forgotten the name of my wedding shoes, but they had Blahnik's signature look: a needle-thin heel and extremely pointy toes. To save on tax, the Barneys salesman suggested I ship both items to my parents' house. A few days later, I got a call from my mother, who was wearing the suit and the shoes. I'd forgotten to tell her that they were coming, and she thought I'd bought them for her.

"You shouldn't have," she said.

"I didn't," I replied.

"The shoes are awfully tight. I think I need a bigger size, and I'm not sure about the pointy toe."

"My mother's been in my wedding shoes," I told Lee. "That's bad luck."

"Who told you that?" he asked.

I had no idea, but I was sure that in some fairy tale a mother wearing her daughter's wedding shoes signaled disaster. Lee bought a pair of Gucci loafers that he considered so expensive he'd forever refer to them as his "special occasion" shoes.

During the ceremony, we were both so nervous we got a bad case of the giggles. When the minister said "for richer or poorer," I thought of our big investment—in Puma shoes—and laughed even harder. The minister looked at us as if we'd both gone crazy, which at least gave us something in common.

Eight years later, when we moved to another apartment with more light but less closet space, Lee finally agreed to get rid of the Puma sneakers. With the emergence of hip-hop, they did become collectors' items, but only the diamond-embossed ones, which he didn't own anyway. We've now been together for thirty-three years. Lee hasn't sprinted away—at least not yet—but whenever we reminisce about the Pumas, I picture a young couple, footloose and fancy-free, and sometimes, when my feet hurt, I miss them.

12

Girlfriend Shoes

I recently donated a pair of gray ostrich flats to a local charity thrift shop. I'd once thought of them as my "lucky shoes," but I hadn't worn them in nearly two decades and every time I saw them in my closet, I felt distinctly unlucky. I figured they deserved a second chance at bringing good fortune to someone else. The thrift shop is within walking distance of my apartment, so I occasionally drop by to see if some crazy rich lady has donated her vast collection of Hermès bags or unworn Louboutin shoes. This has never happened, although I did see a woman trying on my ostrich flats. She must have been in her early eighties and was wearing a fox stole, complete with head and tail. Her feet were much smaller than mine, but since she was wearing thick compression stockings, the shoes seemed to fit. Her friend, who was bedecked in giant cocktail rings and carried a worn Chanel bag, was trying to convince her to buy them.

"They're a bargain," she said. "Authentic python."

"Actually, they're ostrich," I said. "They used to be mine."

I must have looked distraught because the first woman said, "Dear, take them back. I'm sure the store will give you a good price."

"No," I said, "they're meant for you."

The woman was delighted with them, and as she went up to the counter, pulling out her money from a little beaded change purse, the other woman stood behind her, holding her cane.

How sweet, I thought. *Old friends.*

※

For many years, I didn't have a best girlfriend in New York. My bullying experience in high school had left me wary of women, which was why my two best friends were men. I longed for an old-fashioned "steel magnolia," someone I could giggle and gossip with, who'd be there for me through good times and bad, a sister without the baggage, an old friend to grow old with. Although she wasn't Southern, didn't have big hair or a syrupy accent, Steffi was my steel magnolia. Born and raised in Forest Hills, Queens, she was an only child and envied me for having sisters. She loved hearing stories about them. By then, Nancy was in graduate school in Boston, and Emily, after a stint in L.A., was back in my old apartment, working for a jewelry company. Over the years, there was increasing tension between us. After I reclaimed my apartment, she accused me of throwing her out of it, and during her time in L.A., she wouldn't speak to me. Given our significant age difference, I worried about her like a mother and she often reacted to my concern like a put-upon adolescent. I couldn't say anything without irritating her. Though I tried to give her what I thought was good advice about her various boyfriends and career opportunities, she resented my efforts and didn't appreciate what she considered my know-it-all personality.

Steffi, on the other hand, loved that part of me. Though our birthdays were only a month apart, I was the "older" one, and Steffi expected me to have all the answers. We first met through Warren when we were all in L.A. She was there with her then-boyfriend, Ira, who was also a friend of Warren's. The whole gang had gone to NYU undergraduate school together. The Steffi-Ira love story took years to unfold. For Ira, it was love at first sight. For Steffi, who could debate the pros and cons of dishwasher detergent, it was more complicated; she liked him but did she "love" him? And what was love anyway? And would she be happy married? And on and on and on . . .

Eleven years later, she realized she did love him enough to marry him and it was clear Ira wasn't going away. He'd been right to hang in there. Of all the couples I knew, they were the best match, his strength and resolve offsetting her indecisiveness. He saw the world in black and white; she was more nuanced and emotional. Steffi cried when she was happy. She cried when she was sad. Since she resembled one of those saucer-eyed kids in a Margaret Keane painting, you couldn't miss her tears, which welled up in her eyes and appeared to float there like bathwater bubbles.

Steffi's access to her emotions made her a wonderful audience. She was also a great listener, and I should know because, in all modesty, I'm one of the best. You know the person nobody talks to at a party? That's not me. I'm the one listening to some stranger confess his extramarital dalliance with his law partner's associate. I'm the one trying to get a drink from the bartender, who tells me he's wanted to be an actor ever since he played Javert in his sixth-grade production of the children's abridged version of *Les Misérables*. For whatever reason, I emit "listening vibes." People tell me all sorts of weird stuff, even those who should know better. Once, when I was doing a story on Bess Myerson, a former Miss America and New York City commissioner who was under investigation for bribery, she talked to me on the phone one day for nearly eight hours.

"*Really?* How can that be?" Steffi said when I told her the story. Though she'd once worked in fashion and later in TV production, she had a severe case of Crohn's disease, an inflammation of the bowel, and was afraid to get another job. In terms of having a career, she lived vicariously through me, and I never wanted to disappoint her. Steffi loved all my stories, whether they landed on magazine covers or involved Warren's ongoing quest for a girlfriend. We both loved Warren. We especially loved gossiping about him, and because Warren was a bit of a narcissist, he loved that he deserved our gossip. It was a win-win for all of us.

"He's in love with dead movie stars," I'd tell her, and she'd say, "*Really?* How can that be?" When anyone came to interview him about his gallery, he posed next to the life-size poster of Louise Brooks in *Diary of a Lost Girl.* They made a great couple, except for one big problem. "I hope he doesn't actually talk to her," I said, and we laughed, but not in a mean way, because Warren was like a brother to us.

One summer, we all rented a house on Fire Island, where the walls were so thin I could hear Ira snoring at night. As a result, Lee and I skipped a lot of weekends, but one stands out. Someone, probably Warren, began squirting people with a garden hose. Ira grabbed another hose and soon we were in the middle of a gigantic water fight. We all ended up totally drenched and laughed until we cried, especially Steffi. It may sound stupid, but it was an incredibly fun day, one of the best, and I can still picture Steffi, barefoot and in cutoffs, trying to put on her shoes. Suddenly, they felt too tight and she didn't know what had happened.

"How weird," she said. "I wonder if my feet grew."

We wouldn't know the answer until later.

We both had narrow feet. *"Really?* How can that be?" she said when I confided my suspicion that "narrow" was going the way of corsets and crinolines. Nobody else seemed to notice or care. I found it very weird. What if the brassiere industry determined that all breasts were a B cup? Or shirt manufacturers set 15 inches as the standard neck size? At a time when everything is "bespoke," from extra-foam triple-shot soy lattes, to BMWs with 5,000 possible seat combinations, 60 percent of American women claim they can't find the right shoe size. When was *foot* taken out of *footwear*?

It happened around the same time I met Steffi, during the early years of the Reagan administration. Just as Reagan set out to show that we couldn't expect Big Government to meet everyone's needs, he taught us that we couldn't expect shoes to fit everyone's feet. He didn't cry, "Obliterate narrow and wide," the way he implored Gorbachev to "tear down this wall!" But he might as well have. When members of the shoe industry pleaded with him for an import quota on footwear, Reagan, whose father had been a struggling shoe salesman, stood firm with free trade. Today, 99 percent of our shoes are imported. Foreign factories have traditionally kept width at "medium," because shoes are built on expensive and labor-intensive wooden frames known as lasts. By limiting sizes, factories can provide shoe companies with a greater number of styles. It's a win for fashion, if not for feet.

※

In my search for the perfect narrow shoe, I discovered Hélène Arpels, a tiny gem of a store at 470 Park Avenue, where Jackie Onassis was a favored client. (Jackie gravitated toward flats, while Aristotle

Onassis, clearly a secure man, pushed her to buy the highest heels.) The shop was decorated with priceless Chinese furniture and gilded Louis XVI chairs, and on display were the line's signature item— satin court pumps with rhinestones. Hélène Arpels designed all the shoes herself. A model before her marriage to Louis Arpels, of the exclusive jeweler Van Cleef & Arpels, she was a member of the International Best-Dressed List and wore diamonds on the toes of her shoes. After I explained that satin court pumps didn't fit my lifestyle, she instructed a beautiful Chinese saleswoman to show me a pair of loafers in the softest napa leather. "I don't suppose they come in triple A," I said. The saleswoman brought out A, AA, and AAA. I was so thrilled I bought two pairs.

Since Steffi had worked in the garment business, she didn't believe in buying retail, instead picking up her clothes and shoes at sample sales. This was pre-Internet, so I don't even know how she found them, but she'd routinely come back from some grimy warehouse to show me a pair of deeply discounted shoes that otherwise would have cost a fortune. One time, she convinced me to go with her, and I was horrified. A woman nearly wrestled me to the ground over a pair of crocodile loafers, and I swore, "Never again." Afterward, we had lunch at Sarabeth's on Amsterdam Avenue, where in the middle of eating chocolate cake—she had a major sweet tooth— she started to cry. She confessed that she'd recently suffered a miscarriage. Though she hadn't known it at the time, she was pregnant on Fire Island. That's why she hadn't been able to get her swollen feet into her shoes.

"I'm afraid I'm never going to be able to have a baby," she said. "You have a career. You have an exciting life. I just want a child."

At the time, Lee and I weren't married, so even though I was in my mid-thirties, I felt no rush to get pregnant. Since my mother had given birth to Nancy later in life, I didn't share Steffi's sense of urgency. Still, my heart ached for her.

When I left Steffi that afternoon, I took the subway down to the Village, where not far from my old Bleecker Street apartment, I interviewed a thirty-nine-year-old man who was dying of AIDS. The son of a prominent neurologist, he had struggled long and hard over the shame he felt for being gay and how it had impacted his family. Eventually, he found some peace, embarking on a ten-year relationship with another man. Though the relationship ended, he had many friends, a nice apartment, and a job he loved as a tour guide on the Circle Line. Then he developed Kaposi's sarcoma, a rare form of cancer, then meningitis, encephalitis, the list went on. Suddenly, he felt old and wondered if he qualified to sit on the bus seats reserved for senior citizens.

He used a cane to steady his wobbly gait, and walking down the street with him was a slow, torturous process. We kept passing other young men leaning on canes and who looked gray and ashen and ghostly. I remembered walking the same streets with Scott. I also remembered how I practiced "walking away" from him. These men, who were approximately my age and who shared similar dreams, were just trying to muster the strength to walk. "*Really?* How can that be?" Steffi would say when I'd bring back my stories. She thought I was very brave, but I wasn't. The men were brave. I was just a good listener.

Over the next few years, I wrote several pieces on AIDS, sitting next to young men receiving chemotherapy, listening to them talk about their impending deaths. It was hard not to feel overwhelmed. "Is there any good news in the world?" I asked Steffi when I dropped by her apartment one day.

Her big eyes filled with tears. "I'm pregnant," she said.

In 1988, I began writing a biography of the photographer Robert Mapplethorpe, who'd just had a major retrospective at the Whitney Museum of American Art. Several years later, the Corcoran Gallery of Art, in Washington, DC, would cancel an exhibit of his controversial work, ultimately leading to the 1991 obscenity trial in Cincinnati. Mapplethorpe's subjects were flowers, portraits, and gay S&M sex. To be equally adept at taking pictures of lilies and of men hanging upside down in chains is a singular talent that gave him a unique edge. Mapplethorpe had AIDS, and in the seven months before he died, at forty-two, I spent hours interviewing him as well as practically everyone he knew. You'd be hard-pressed to find a more eclectic group, from art collectors and socialites to men who kept dungeons in their apartments and embraced every fetish imaginable.

Though Steffi had given birth to her daughter, Pamela, and was happier than I'd ever seen her, she still hadn't lost any of her curiosity and still expected me to provide the answers.

"You're telling me that people can have orgasms licking people's toes?" she asked.

"It's called a foot fetish," I said, "and it's not just licking people's toes. Lots of men are into women's shoes, the higher the better."

One of Mapplethorpe's models had worked as a call girl and told me that she frequently dealt with foot fetishists. Several of her regulars, including the president of a major U.S. corporation, would lick her shoes for hours at a time. She said it was so boring she grew to hate the man. I showed Steffi a Mapplethorpe photo of an African-American model about to put a patent-leather lime-green heel into his open mouth.

"That is really very weird," she said.

"For some people, heels are symbols of cruelty and pain, and that's a turn-on."

"I bet women don't have foot fetishes," she said.

"Why?" I asked.

"Just having to wear high heels is cruel and painful enough."

We laughed and then played with Pamela, who had just come home from nursery school.

"I think you should have a baby," Steffi said suddenly. "It would make you so happy."

Once Lee and I finally got married, we tried to have a baby, but who knew that getting pregnant at forty would be difficult? Obviously, I did because I'd written about it, but stories about other people are exactly that: stories about other people.

I made an appointment with my gynecologist, whom I'd never really liked but who'd been my doctor when I'd had my breast biopsy. Since it turned out to be benign, I was too superstitious to leave him, though I always thought it weird that he kept a bronze figurine of two copulating tortoises on his desk. After I'd researched the mating habits of tortoises, I wasn't sure what this said about his approach to sex, since the male tortoise bites, butts, rams, and shell-batters the female into submission.

After I complained that I was feeling depressed because it seemed that every man I met had AIDS, he wanted to know why I was dating men with AIDS. He hoped they wore condoms. As for getting pregnant, he advised me to relax and give it a year. Looking at the copulating tortoises, I thought, "Slow and steady wins the race."

My book was proceeding slowly and steadily. I'd finished most of the interviews but wanted to see Mapplethorpe's gravesite in Queens.

Since I'd never driven in the city and had no idea how to get to Queens, I asked Steffi if she'd take me to the cemetery and then we could have lunch afterward. "We can go to the grave and then Sarabeth's," I said.

It was a cold, gray day, and it took us forever to find the gravesite. Mapplethorpe's ashes had been placed next to his mother's coffin, and the headstone bore his mother's maiden name.

"So now what?" Steffi said.

"I guess we can drive back to the city and have lunch."

At Sarabeth's, I told her nothing was happening on the pregnancy front, and Steffi's eyes immediately filled up with tears. I don't cry easily but she got me started, and we both cried together. Her tears fell into a slice of chocolate cake, mine into a cappuccino. She suggested that maybe we should go shopping. In my current state, I told her I couldn't possibly handle a sample sale, but she said, "Trust me, I know a good one." So we drove to a decrepit warehouse in midtown, where I found the gray ostrich flats—in narrow. I viewed them as good luck charms and wore them practically every day. I'd read that Chinese women trying to conceive would take a shoe from the temple of the fertility goddess, and then after the child arrived, the mother would return the shoe. I'd made a bargain that if I got pregnant, I'd give away the ostrich flats. I also kept thinking of the nursery rhyme about the old woman who lived in a shoe and who had so many children she didn't know what to do. In all the illustrations, she had gray hair and appeared to be in her eighties, so maybe there was hope for me.

Eventually, my gynecologist referred me to a fertility specialist, who suggested artificial insemination, along with the drug Pergonal. It had to be injected beneath your skin every day for three weeks. I hate needles and I'm very drug sensitive. The Pergonal made me a little crazy and I began to cry every time Lee administered the shot.

When I returned to the specialist's office with a vial of Lee's sperm in my pocketbook, I put on a hospital gown, climbed atop the examining table, and placed my feet in the stirrups.

"Don't you want to take off your shoes?" the nurse asked.

"No, they're lucky."

After the doctor completed the insemination, he told me that for the next thirty minutes, I should do nothing but think calming thoughts. I focused on the shoes, concluding that gray really is the perfect neutral. I counted the number of bumps on the ostrich skin. I wondered if ostriches built nests and where. I hoped an ostrich hadn't been killed to make my shoes. I started feeling bad for ostriches, so I reached for one of the pamphlets on the wall rack. It was all about the benefits of cosmetic breast surgery. Doesn't a woman who is trying to get pregnant have problems enough without worrying about her breast size?

When the doctor returned and asked if I'd had a "nice rest," I waved the brochure at him. "This is an insult to women," I said.

The double insult?

I didn't get pregnant.

I went to another fertility doctor for more shots of Pergonal, only to develop a bad case of pneumonia. When I recovered, I went to yet another fertility doctor to see about doing in vitro. It wasn't as advanced as it is now, so I was a little apprehensive. After he reviewed several months of blood tests, he told me the bad news: I didn't have a chance in hell of getting pregnant because my follicle-stimulating hormone, which is released by the pituitary gland, was so high I was heading into menopause.

"But I've never missed a period," I explained, baffled.

"It doesn't matter," he said. "I guarantee that in a month or two, you'll be in menopause."

"But my mother didn't go into menopause until she was fifty-four," I insisted. "Isn't there a correlation?"

"Often there is," he said. "But in your case, no."

I couldn't believe what I'd heard. Not only was there no baby in my future, but I was going into menopause at forty-one. I immediately called Steffi. "That's ridiculous," she said. "You're so physically sensitive that you'd be the first person to know if you were heading into menopause."

She was right. Just like my mother, I didn't reach menopause until I was fifty-four.

But that still doesn't mean I got pregnant.

⚘

In typical Steffi fashion, one morning she called to ask my advice on clowns.

"Why would you think I'd know about clowns?" I asked.

"You always have the answers to things, and I was thinking that maybe you'd written a story about a circus and had met a clown."

She then launched into Pamela's "clown problem." Apparently, they petrified her. I didn't think it was such a big deal, but Steffi reminded me that clowns appeared regularly at kids' birthday parties. Also, one of Steffi's relatives wore so much makeup she looked like a clown, and Pamela didn't want to see her. Steffi asked if I'd discuss Pamela's clown issue with my therapist, who explained that fear of clowns was in fact a real psychological problem. It even had a name—coulrophobia. She suggested that Steffi take Pamela to see someone, but the clown phobia went away, or else the relative did. I can't remember.

At some point, I suggested to Steffi that she should see a therapist because dealing with the ups and downs of her Crohn's disease was taking its toll. It never occurred to Steffi that she'd actually have to *talk* to the therapist. She was more interested in listening to him. "He wants me to bring him dreams," she said. "I don't remember any. Can you tell me some of yours?"

"That would defeat the purpose," I explained.

"So maybe you could give me a few examples?"

After I described several of my dreams, she told me her therapist thought she might be having some sexual issues.

"Like what?" I asked.

"He wonders why all this S&M imagery keeps cropping up."

"That's because you've been listening to me talk about Mapplethorpe."

"And because I've been using your dreams as mine," she confessed.

"Steffi, you can't do that. You need your own dreams."

But she had hers—Pamela. She'd recite a poem Pamela had written or tell me something funny Pamela had said. She worried that it might make me feel bad, but it didn't. I totally shared in her joy.

On February 23, 1994, Warren called me early in the morning. Warren never called early. We usually spoke at lunchtime. "Are you sitting down?" he said. That's a sentence you never want to hear because it implies that the news you are about to hear is so awful it might cause you to collapse.

"Steffi's gone," he said.

"What do you mean? I spoke to her last night."

He explained in a flat voice that she'd been taken to the hospital, where she'd died of septic shock, a rare complication of Crohn's disease. He'd just accompanied a devastated Ira to the morgue to identify the body. Steffi was only forty-three; Pamela had just turned eight. The funeral service was so wrenchingly sad, it pains me to look back on it. Ira was in total shock. Pamela, all dressed up, a grief-stricken little doll, sat next to him. No one could believe Steffi was dead. I remember wearing the ostrich shoes. I also remember that I never wore them again.

I recently had dinner with Pamela, who is now twenty-nine and who looks a lot like her mother. They have the same big brown eyes that tear easily. She reminds me of Steffi in other ways too. She's kind and sensitive and a good listener. She has a successful career and recently became engaged to a wonderful man. They've set the wedding date for next fall, and of course I'll buy new shoes. Warren, Woody, and all my friends, except one, will be there. I know I'll laugh. I know I'll cry, and I know at some point I'll hear Steffi's voice whisper, *"Really?* How can that be?" And this time I won't have an answer.

13

Go-Go Boots

$\mathcal{L}$ ee and I celebrated our fifteenth wedding anniversary in London. He said I could pick out any present (within reason) and I selected a pair of brown leather lace-up ankle boots at Emma Hope, in Notting Hill. Hope designed Keira Knightley's shoes for *Pride and Prejudice* and her tagline—"regalia for feet"—conjures up a festive regency ball. Though my boots weren't silk or velvet, or embellished with tassels or appliqués, with their small tapered heel and elongated toe, they had a distinct Victorian charm that meant the world to me.

Hope, who opened her first shop when she was only twenty-five, fell in love with vintage pieces, scouring flea markets for items she could revive and rework. She's often said that she finds her inspiration in "granny's closet," a phrase that resonated with me because, even though both my grandmothers died before I was born, I've often drawn inspiration from them too.

For years my father kept a small sepia photograph of his mother on his bureau. I'd always admired it. She has lovely blue eyes, a straight nose, and thick brown hair piled on top of her head in the "Gibson girl" style. He rarely speaks about her, and even though I've spent my life posing questions to strangers, I intuited from an early age that she was off-limits. She died too young, and it was simply too painful, and yet I see my father in her eyes and I see myself in them too.

My maternal grandmother, Bumpa's wife, lived until her late sixties, yet she was even more of a mystery. My mother didn't have much to say about her, and I can only chalk it up to my mother's reluctance to ask questions. Her curiosity mainly extended to pets. She was crazy about them and knew the names of all the neighbors' animals. Her greatest hope was that I'd write a children's book about dogs or cats, though she was leaning toward cats.

"You're so imaginative," she said. "It's too bad you're wasting your time with all this other stuff."

The "other stuff" was a successful journalism career, but I'd learned not to take her comments personally. "I think you could write a wonderful story about a group of magical cats with human characteristics," she'd once advised.

I told her that was a ridiculous idea, and then *Cats* came along and my mother said she couldn't listen to Betty Buckley sing "Memories" without thinking of all the royalties we could have split.

Every time I tried to steer her away from four-legged creatures toward my two-legged grandmother, she'd draw a total blank. "I wasn't nosy like you," she said. "In those days, we were brought up to be polite."

"So you can't even describe her?"

"She was an excellent seamstress."

"And?"

"A devout Catholic."

"That's it?"

"Oh, and she had thinning hair and wore what they used to call a rat to plump it up."

"You paint such a fascinating portrait."

"I'm sorry, but we all can't live your fascinating life."

The only problem with my mother's vague description was that at one point, my grandmother did indeed live a fascinating life. On the top shelf of Bumpa's closet, I discovered three frayed photo albums that provided a rich if cryptic visual biography. My grandmother brought them to New York from her native London, where, in 1903, she'd embarked on a seven-year journey around the world. For someone who'd once considered Cape Cod the Phuket of Greater Boston, I treated the albums as if they were tales from *The Arabian Nights*. Only there weren't any tales—just pictures of my grandmother, a tall, dark-haired woman with a penchant for big hats and a collection of fabulous shoes. One pair was particularly gorgeous: white Louis-heeled court shoes with little bows. Her shoe collection took her everywhere—India, Egypt, Japan, Hong Kong, China, Burma, Thailand, the Caribbean, Washington, New York, Newport, and, finally, Andover. She traveled by ocean liner, horse, camel, and oxcart, posing next to Japanese geishas, the Great Buddha in Kamakura, near battleships in Vancouver, the Palace of the Winds in Jaipur, the Great Sphinx in Giza. For years I made up my own story about her life. Depending on what I was reading, she was an adventuress like Gertrude Bell, a maharajah's mistress, a British spy, the grand duchess Anastasia. Some pictures had been ripped out of the albums, but since they'd been glued onto the page, the perpetrator had left behind remnants. From what I could tell, the pictures had been of a man. A lover? A first husband?

Somehow en route to New York, my grandmother lost her steamer trunk and arrived at Ellis Island with only the things she carried with her. Among them was a gold trinket in the shape of a shoe. Victorians often exchanged miniature shoes in leather or pottery. It was a symbol of a contented, prosperous life. Did she view it as a good luck charm? A fertility symbol? Or a reminder that she loved shoes? My mother kept it in a small curio cabinet in the basement, next to a Ping-Pong table nobody ever used. She was very possessive of the few things in it, though she rarely looked at them. One day I slipped the shoe trinket into my pocket and brought it back with me to New York, where I placed it on a delicate gold chain. It symbolized all the places I'd been and the ones I still wanted to see.

⁂

With my new Emma Hope boots, I began to wander like a tourist through my grandmother's life. Lee had several meetings, so I used the time to do a little digging at various research centers in London. Since I already knew her childhood address from the Ellis Island website, I took the tube to Great Titchfield Street, in Marylebone. *So this is where your grand adventure began*, I thought, walking past rows of redbrick Victorian houses. When I reached her block, there were no more charming houses, just a hideous modern building. My grandmother's address was now the Winchester Club, where a sign advertised a MEMBERS ONLY party: SUMMER SNACKS, BLACKJACK, AND THE MALIBU GIRLS GROOVING THE NIGHT AWAY.

A man came out and saw me taking notes. "Looking for some-one?" he asked.

"Yeah," I said. "My grandmother."

He looked skeptical. "In *here*?"

After more research, I discovered that my grandmother had been a lady's maid to several socially prominent women whose husbands were in politics, both in England and the United States. My grandmother's career as a domestic was the last thing my mother wanted to hear and she told me that if I'd stuck to cats, none of this would have come to light. Still, I persisted and discovered something I hoped she'd find interesting: In addition to being Irish and English, we were also part French.

"Your great-grandmother's name was Eugénie Sherrier," I announced proudly. "She married Alphonse Rousset, and they had a daughter named Lucie—your grandmother."

"Did Alphonse have an interesting career?" she asked.

"He worked as a glazier."

My mother turned up her nose. "What's that?"

After I explained that it was somebody who installed glass, she said, "Like a construction worker?"

"But listen, your grandmother Lucie was a midwife. In another era, she might have been a doctor."

"But she wasn't," my mother said. "So for all your snooping, you've unearthed a construction worker, a midwife, and a maid. I thought you said this was going to be interesting."

"I think it is."

"Interesting would be if Eugénie had been Empress Eugénie."

"I think we'd know it if your mother had been married to Napoleon III," I said.

"You never know."

"I would."

"Oh, right, you know everything. You're French."

☙

Apart from their annual two-week vacation at the beach, my parents rarely went anywhere. They'd been out of the country only once, for their honeymoon in Quebec.

Over the years, I've been fortunate to travel for work and pleasure, and when I thought of my mother in my Manolo Blahnik wedding shoes, I realized that she yearned for the excitement and freedom the shoes represented. Her mother and daughter had traveled. Why couldn't she? But with Nancy coming along so late in their lives, and my father still paying her college tuition, expensive vacations were out of the question.

But then something wonderful happened: frequent-flyer miles. Unlike now, when the airlines make it nearly impossible to cash them in, at one point, they were like free money. Lee traveled a lot for business, and since we couldn't use all the miles he'd accumulated, we transferred them to my parents. Once we even gave them the highly coveted "Anywhere in the World" award, hoping they'd take full advantage and pick some distant exotic place. With a choice of anywhere in the world, my mother chose Disney World.

"It's not a real world," I explained. "It's a fantasy world."

"What's wrong with that?" she asked.

"Nothing, except this is a big award, and you might as well go someplace really far away."

"Disney World is far away. It's where dreams are born."

"You're thinking of Neverland."

"Which I can see at Disney World."

So my parents went to Disney World, and my mother, having whetted her appetite for foreign countries at Epcot, was ready to broaden her horizons. They went to London; they went to Italy twice; they toured Ireland, once with us to celebrate their fiftieth wedding anniversary. By then, they were such old hands that after they finished unpacking at our hotel in Connemara, they went to the bar for a predinner drink. We found them talking to a couple who just happened to live two floors above us in our New York apartment

building. "Small world," my mother said, even though hers kept
expanding.

When they were nearly eighty, my parents went to Paris. My
mother asked my advice on what to pack and I told her definitely no
sneakers. "That's a giveaway that you're a tourist," I said. But my
mother reminded me that she *was* a tourist, and if shop clerks and
waiters were fooled into thinking she was French by looking at her
shoes, they'd know she wasn't the minute she opened her mouth. She
had a good point. Why do we think sneakers are going to give us
away as "Ugly Americans" when plenty of Parisians are walking
around in them? It's true they look much better in them, and they
don't wear them with shorts, athletic socks, and baseball caps, but
sneakers are the least of our fashion problems.

My mother brought sneakers, along with her jeans. For years
she'd hated jeans, thinking that only hippies and drug addicts wore
them, and then when she reached her seventies, you couldn't get her
out of them. Her favorites came from a local store named Appleseed's, which she insisted on calling Johnny Appleseed, after the legendary pioneer who planted apple trees throughout the United States.
The store's motto: Classic is ageless. And indeed my mother's jeans
were "classic" in that they were never in style, so they were never out
of style. To call them Mom jeans would indicate that they had an
unfashionable shape, when they actually had no shape at all. They
were like denim sweatpants, but since she was so tall and thin, they
looked cute on her.

Lee managed to get business-class tickets, which my mother kept
referring to as "businessman's class." She thought it was the height of
glamour, and from then on, coach was a total comedown. After an
overnight flight and no sleep, my parents spent the entire day walking around the Right Bank, before hopping on a Paris by Night Illu-

minations bus tour. My mother had the best time of her life. She loved the city's architecture. She loved the fashion. She didn't love the food because she's a picky eater but loved that she lost five pounds. She bought herself a pair of knockoff Chanel ballet flats and me an illustrated children's book on cats—*Le Livre du Pays des Chats*.

In the 1990s, we rented a series of summer homes in East Hampton, where my parents would always spend a week. My mother loved the Hamptons and urged us to buy a house before prices rose too high. "You'll regret it," she said, "like you did with *Cats*."

Traveling was one of the best things that ever happened to my mother. It made her feel more confident, as if she finally had something in common with her own mother. She still didn't remember a lot of details about her, though after she spotted the gold shoe around my neck, she remembered that I'd taken it and wanted it back.

"It was given to her by her first love," she said.

"Was he the man she ripped out of the albums?" I asked.

"Yes. His name was Jack."

"Jack the Ripper?"

"Patricia, that's a horrible thing to say about your grandmother. I can assure you that she didn't date Jack the Ripper."

"Yeah, because she'd have been dead."

"Can I please have my gold charm back?"

Naturally, I gave it to her. She'd earned her traveling shoes.

14

In the Heights

When I moved to the Upper West Side in 1976, I received a lot of unwanted attention from a drug addict who lived in Verdi Square, across from the 72nd Street subway station. Named after the Italian composer Giuseppe Verdi, it was more famous as Needle Park, a popular destination for drug users and dealers, as well as the setting for *The Panic in Needle Park,* starring a very young Al Pacino. Except for the needle dangling from his arm, my drug addict looked nothing like Pacino, though he did have the actor's talent for over-the-top line readings. Despite his addled condition, he still managed to summon his full vocal power to comment on my appearance as I raced to the subway each morning. "Your ass looks *waaaay* too big in those pants," he'd yell. "Or no *waaaay* is red your color."

Before long, I was factoring his slurred comments into my daily wardrobe routine. This was absurd for many reasons, not the least of which was the man's own style, which relied heavily on cardboard, plaid rags, and a floral nightgown fashioned into a kilt. Once he called me over to where he was lying in a pool of his own urine to inquire if he could ask a "personal question." Since his good manners offset his vile odor, I agreed. Pointing to my brown suede loafers, he said, "You're never gonna get a man in those things! They're *waaaay* too ugly!"

Since this happened right after I'd split up with Scott, I was feeling particularly vulnerable. Were my loafers a turnoff to men? As I waited for the subway, I wondered why was I taking fashion advice from a homeless drug addict. Was I that insecure?

The answer, I'm sorry to say, is yes. Which brings me to my love/hate relationship with high heels. I love the way they look but hate the way they feel. I wish it were otherwise. I wish I could run, skip, and jump in five-inch platforms, but I can't. I'm convinced few women can, only they fake it better. Or maybe it means more to them than it does to me, but since I'm writing this book, you've got to figure it means quite a bit.

My limit is two inches, maybe three, but even that turns me into the martyred Crispin and Crispinian, the patron saints of shoemakers. Crispin and Crispinian were possibly brothers, maybe even twins, or most probably fiction. (During Vatican II, they were "delisted" as saints.) Crispin, whose feast day falls on October 25, is the more famous brother, thanks to Shakespeare's *Henry V* and its inspiring St. Crispin's Day speech. Henry, heavily outnumbered, rouses his troops to fight the French at Agincourt, uttering the celebrated lines "We few, we happy few, we band of brothers."

Depending on the source, Crispin and Crispinian were French or part Italian and British. They made shoes at night and preached Christianity during the day, which prompted the Romans to devise various tortures to force them to recant their faith, including drowning, burning, and placing them on the rack. If the brothers had lived in the 1990s, the Romans could have placed them in Vivienne Westwood's nine-inch platforms—the very shoes that caused supermodel Naomi Campbell's infamous catwalk tumble—and forced them to sprint up and down the Spanish Steps.

For most of my life, I avoided the high-heel dilemma. I was too young for the stiletto craze of the 1950s; I embraced the flat styles of the sixties; I ignored the platforms of the seventies; and during the eighties, I wore low-heeled pumps with my broad-shouldered "power suits," which in retrospect were ridiculous and made me look like Joan Crawford. Still, I could walk. And then, in the early nineties, grunge came along and ruined everything for me.

The style emerged from the scrappy garage band scene in Seattle, where it was linked to Nirvana frontman Kurt Cobain, who mixed lumberjack clothes with feminine floral prints. Cobain, a heroin addict, later committed suicide but not before marrying Courtney Love, who was also addicted to heroin and who popularized the "kinder-whore" look—torn Baby Doll dresses, cigarette-burned stockings, smudged makeup, and Mary Janes or military boots. For his spring 1993 collection, Marc Jacobs, who was then creative director of Perry Ellis, sent Christy Turlington, Kate Moss, and former first lady of France, Carla Bruni-Sarkozy, down the runway in fashion's version of grunge. The models wore plaid-printed "lumberjack" silks, thermal cashmere sweaters, crocheted beanies, and chunky Doc Martens, which had been a symbol of urban rebellion long before Nirvana. Skinheads wore them. Punks wore them. Malcolm McDowell and his fellow droogs wore them in *A Clockwork Orange*. Elton John wore a giant pair as the Pinball Wizard in the Who's *Tommy*. I'd have worn them too because they looked comfortable, but grunge wasn't for me.

It also wasn't for the executives at Perry Ellis who promptly fired

Jacobs. Why did women need to spend a lot of money on Salvation Army–inspired clothes when they could go directly to the Salvation Army? In retrospect, my drug addict, with his fondness for floral and plaid, was into grunge long before it even had a name. He may well have invented it.

As a reaction to grunge's androgyny and lack of sales appeal, a new trend emerged, one drawn from "Girl Power," which was a rebuke to 1970s feminism, or, as writer Naomi Wolf labeled it, victim feminism. The "postfeminist" woman could be girlish and powerful. She could present herself as a sex object because she was "owning" it, along with something else: shoes. The stiletto was the weapon of choice for the new power-seeking, sexually assertive female. Though many designers adopted the trend, Tom Ford received the most attention for his modern interpretation of 1970s decadent glamour. Integral to the look were extreme shoes, such as metal-heeled stilettos with bondage leg ties. Collaborating with photographer Mario Testino and stylist/muse Carine Roitfeld, the designer helped create an eye-catching ad campaign that promoted his "porno chic" aesthetic. Though not as perversely shocking as Guy Bourdin's 1970s photos for shoemaker Charles Jourdan—one showed the outline of a body on a blood-splattered pavement—they presented the merchandise in a violent, sexually charged way.

Anyone who has ever worn high heels or watched anybody walk in them knows how they emphasize a woman's anatomy, pushing out her breasts, elevating her butt, and making her hips swivel. According to the scientific journal *Evolution and Human Behavior*, it's the reason men prefer women in heels. The authors go on to compare these women to "female baboons with a larger than normal swelling of the bottom associated with the sexually receptive period of their cycle." This led me to google *ovulating baboon*, and I wish I hadn't.

A picture showed the baboon's bottom not only greatly engorged but bright red. In 2008, social psychologists at the University of Rochester conducted a study that concluded that men found women dressed in red more attractive than ones wearing chromatic colors like green and blue. In their sexual response to women, they are not far removed from baboons. They like big bottoms and they like red.

Female activist Beatrice Faust believes that high heels are not just a turn-on for men. By making the buttocks undulate twice as much, they spread sexual sensations throughout a woman's body. Since I've never walked far enough in high heels to experience multiple undulations, I'll have to take her word for it.

My plan was to ride out the stiletto craze until fashion reversed itself, but the popularity of *Sex and the City* made that impossible. The show was a paean to shoes, turning Manolo Blahnik and Jimmy Choo into superstars. Designer high heels had never been so highly coveted, which made my World Is Flat theory seem totally archaic.

Finally, I broke down and bought a pair of three-inch Manolo Blahnik Carolyne slingback pumps. They were created in the 1980s for the former fashion designer Carolyne Roehm, who was then married to billionaire financier Henry Kravis and lived in an opulent Park Avenue duplex. That is not the reason I bought the shoes. I bought them because they were classic. "I'll have them forever," I told Lee, who said, "No, you won't, because you won't be able to walk in them." If Carolyne Roehm could walk in them, I could. Of course, Roehm had a car and driver, but at some point even Carolyne had to walk in her Carolynes.

❦

For centuries, shoes have been a mark of wealth and status, high heels elevating aristocrats far above the crowd. When the heel was first invented in the sixteenth century, it wasn't economically feasible for cobblers to make "paired" lasts for right and left. Instead of giving up their heels, people preferred to wear "straight" shoes that over time conformed to their feet. In France during the eighteenth century, Louis XIV made the red heel—the *talon rouge*—a symbol of nobility; only members of his court were allowed to wear them, as long as they were lower than the king's. With its concave curve and outward taper at the base, the Louis heel became very popular with women, until the French Revolution put an end to any outward sign of ostentation, and flats returned to fashion.

With this in mind, I approached my Carolynes from the perspective of someone lucky enough to live in an era when I didn't have to sacrifice left for right or worry about losing my head. Marie Antoinette would have loved Blahnik, which is probably why Sofia Coppola chose him to design the shoes for her movie about the French queen. His styles tend to run small and narrow, with a pointy toe box. This lends the illusion of small, dainty feet, which men are said to prefer, even though some of the world's sexiest women, such as Angelina Jolie, Uma Thurman, Heidi Klum, and Charlize Theron, wear size 9 and larger. In China, the tiny foot was so highly prized that it led to the practice of foot binding, which involved breaking all the toes, except the big one, and then continually wrapping tight cloth around the foot. The result was the aesthetically pleasing "lotus" shape, which like genital mutilation was thought essential for a good marriage. When foot binding went out of fashion in the nineteenth century, many husbands abandoned their wives for the same reason they'd married them.

❦

My first outing in my new Carolynes took place at Lincoln Center, where the film society was paying tribute to the star of *The Panic in*

Needle Park—Al Pacino, who, coincidentally, once worked as a shoe salesman. After the tribute, there was a dinner at Tavern on the Green, which involved walking from Avery Fisher Hall across Broadway and Columbus, down West 65th Street, across Central Park West, and into the park. I know you're supposed to "break in" new shoes before wearing them, but whenever I hear that phrase, I think of the scene in *The Misfits* when Clark Gable breaks the wild mustang so he can sell it to a dog food manufacturer. Marilyn Monroe is so poignant as she tries to stop him that I've long since forgiven her for helping to make high heels a standard for feminine beauty.

By the time I reached Broadway and West 65th Street, I realized that my Carolynes were breaking me. "You go ahead," I called to Woody and Warren and their wives. (Warren was now married to a vivacious former CEO and they would soon have two children.)

"I thought you said they were comfortable," Lee reminded me. "You said they were classics."

"They are classics, but classic is different than comfortable, and my toes are getting squished."

We stopped in the middle of the block, where I pulled off my right shoe in front of a mountain of black garbage bags. As I balanced on one foot, I felt something scurry across my left shoe. I looked down. It was a huge rat. If Lee hadn't grabbed my elbow, I'd have fallen headfirst into the mound of garbage. I tried to imagine the rat as a benevolent Disney rodent, like the sweet mice that helped Cinderella redesign her ball gown, but it was too disgusting. I managed to reach Tavern on the Green but couldn't forget the sensation of the rat's tail brushing against my ankle. From then on, my Carolynes no longer evoked the image of an ex–fashion designer and society hostess, but one of those inflatable rats with gigantic teeth and scabby bellies that unions place in front of buildings to protest employment practices. No heel had ever come down to earth so quickly. When Lee began referring to them as Carolyne the Rat Shoes, I knew that Carolyne and I had to split up. They were my trophy heels, and while I couldn't offer them a hefty settlement, I could give them a nice funeral, shrouding them in their white shoe bag before placing them in their Blahnik boxed coffin. They're now safely interred on the top shelf of my closest, next to my Lucchese Western boots, which I haven't worn since 1979, and probably never will.

✻

In 2004, Tom Ford left Gucci, and I for one couldn't have been happier. He was going to Hollywood to make films, and unless they were sequels to *Sex and the City,* I felt confident that he'd leave women's feet alone. By then, however, the Cult of the High Heel had firmly taken hold. Ford's muse, Carine Roitfeld, who was famous for her bondage stilettos, had become editor of French *Vogue.* With the growing popularity of street-style photography, Roitfeld was impossible to escape, striding confidently from one fashion show to another in dominatrix footwear that soon became standard wear for other editors, retailers, stylists, celebrities, and fashion-conscious women everywhere.

"A shoe has so much more to offer than just to walk," Christian Louboutin told *The New Yorker.* Indeed, locomotion has very little to do with the Louboutin aesthetic, which takes its cue from traditional fetish wear. Though Louboutin had been making shoes since the early 1990s, he didn't achieve widespread recognition until he introduced his Very Prive platform in 2006. With its aggressive contours and nearly five-inch heel, the Very Prive transformed its wearer into a tower of kinkiness. A year later, Louboutin collaborated with *Twin Peaks* creator David Lynch on Fetish, a darkly twisted photographic exhibit featuring a pair of naked women posed like German artist Hans Bellmer's erotic dolls. The models wore shoes with vertiginous metal heels, including one pair—the Siamese—that was actually fused together.

Louboutin's signature red soles proved to be a brilliant marketing device, at once eye-catching and uniquely Louboutin. They made a statement about social status and sexual allure, telegraphing to the world that the wearer was rich, sexy, and possibly even ovulating. What other shoe designer could make you think of both Louis XIV and a fertile baboon?

Louboutin's shoes became increasingly taller, decorated with studs, fur, fabric, and glitter. They were magical, beautiful, ugly, and weird, but it took the fashion genius Alexander McQueen to make the highest, most bizarre-looking shoes since Gene Simmons debuted his dragon-inspired, silver-scaled demon boots for KISS's 1976 Destroyer tour. While McQueen's booties didn't have metal teeth embellishing the toe, they did have twelve-inch crustacean claws. The Armadillo booties were part of his spring 2010 collection, Plato's Atlantis, which represented his interpretation of Darwin's *Origin of Species*. In this case, however, the models, in reptilian silk-screened prints, appeared to be de-evolving back into the sea. Four months later, McQueen, who'd struggled with drugs and depression, committed suicide. The Armadillo shoes, however, live on in legend and in Lady Gaga's video for her single "Bad Romance."

๛

I began to notice that the Cult of the High Heel, especially the high-heeled sandal, required certain time-consuming rituals, such as regular pedicures. I've always been wary of nail salons for fear of picking up a nail fungus. Back in the days when I thought I might enjoy getting pedicures, I purchased my own personal utensil box, but now it's so old it's probably the most unsanitary thing in the salon. My sister Nancy loves getting pedicures and thinks it's the most relaxing experience. When I go to the nail salon, only in the summer and under great duress, I watch other women lean back in ecstasy while someone pounds their lower legs, pulls their toes, and pummels their heels. And that's just the massage part. Before that, you have to endure scrubbing, scraping, cutting, clipping, and the confusing task of "picking a color." Even little girls know the lingo. "I want Essie's Turquoise and Caicos mixed with Opi's Ski Teal We Drop," they'll say, while I'll mumble, "Just something natural." The nail technicians always looked disappointed. "Don't you want something exciting, like Essie's Russian Roulette?" they'll ask. "It's a very nice red." But I don't want red, and if I did, I could buy Louboutin's Rouge, which is inspired by the red on the soles of his shoes. The seven-inch "stiletto" cap is modeled after the heel of his Ballerina Ultima shoe, and if they ever do *Basic Instinct 3*, I have the perfect weapon for Sharon Stone.

In my limited nail salon experience, I've noticed that women who are obsessed with pedicures tend to have ugly feet because they're usually obsessed with high heels. If worn often enough, heels can cause unsightly bunions, corns, calluses, hyperextended joints, big toes that mimic the pointy shape of a stiletto, and "pump bump," a bony enlargement on the back of the heel. (They can also cause back pain and osteoarthritis, but I'm focusing on the visuals.) What's the point of wearing high heels to look sexy if your feet are anything but? You can attempt to disguise the problem by wearing something dark and dramatic, like Essie's Devil's Advocate, but as Al Pacino, who played Satan in that movie, said, "*HAHAHA!*"

Over the past decade, enterprising podiatrists have come up with ways to correct ugly feet, which not only have to support the full weight of your body but have to look beautiful doing it. These various methods have been called the Foot Face-Lift or Cinderella Surgery, which is a misnomer because Cinderella fit into the glass slipper. In the Brothers Grimm version, it was the Ugly Stepsisters who couldn't squeeze into the shoe, so one cut off her toe, the other her heel. The prince was not fooled. But in this new blend of medicine and fable, anyone can have "designer feet for designer shoes." There's aesthetic toe shortening and toe lengthening for what one podiatrist has called the Perfect 10, fat suctioning for "toebesity," and injectable fillers to plump up the bottoms of the feet to make walking on them less painful. If all else fails, there are always painkillers, including the nerve blocker Marcaine.

Or you could just wear comfortable, well-fitting shoes. I once interviewed a foot model for a story that had nothing to do with feet. It was about how real estate prices were pushing creative young people out of Manhattan and into places they didn't want to go, like Brooklyn. (At the time, this was considered tragic.) When I met the model, she was sitting with her legs up, her feet covered in a thick moisturizer and swaddled in layers of Saran Wrap. When I asked her what she thought of her new neighborhood, she said she really didn't know because she never walked around it. At some point during the interview, she pulled off the plastic, wiped off the moisturizer, and showed me her feet. They were beautiful. A Perfect 10.

"On the rare occasions when you do walk," I asked, "what kind of shoes do you wear?"

"Sneakers with thick socks," she said.

"Even at night."

"Even at night."

I remember thinking, *There's a lesson to be learned here.*

And then I promptly forgot it.

✿

A few years ago, I was asked to do a story on Gucci, which brought up my conflicted feelings about Tom Ford, who was now back in the fashion business, though not at Gucci. Still, it was hard to escape Ford's influence on the "Gucci woman" as someone whose feet were molded onto stilettos. I'd been invited to attend the Gucci Women in Cinema Awards in Venice, a city famous for its exaggerated footwear. In the early sixteenth century, noblewomen wore "chopines," which were extremely high platforms that could be anywhere from five to nine inches off the ground. (The Correr Museum, in St. Mark's Square, has a twenty-inch pair.) Chopines, which were kept hidden under a woman's skirt, highlighted a woman's wealth, as well as her sumptuous clothing. Though she rarely left her palazzo, when she did venture out for a formal event, she often needed servants to help her navigate. Walking was even more difficult for the officially sanctioned courtesans, who had access to the nobility and were expected to dress like upper-class women, including wearing chopines.

Whenever I think of courtesans, I can't help thinking of the couture collector, society hostess, and inveterate partygoer Nan Kempner, whom I'd met in Venice many years ago. At one point, the conversation turned to the limited choices afforded to Venetian women: courtesan or nun. She immediately said that she'd be a courtesan. "Think of the sex. The fun!" Thinking of the chopines, I opted for nun.

The second time I ran into Kempner, I was recovering from a bad knee injury after a gang of teenagers assaulted me in Central Park. En route to Venice, our plane crash-landed in Brussels, and I had to slide down the emergency chute in my knee brace. Several hours later, badly shaken and without our luggage, Lee and I checked into our hotel and immediately bumped into Kempner. Ignoring our disheveled state, she got straight to the point. "Are you free for dinner?" she asked. I explained that we'd just been in a plane crash.

"Well, that's all in the past," she said.

"Actually, it was only four hours ago."

"Shall we say eightish?"

The only shoes I brought with me were sturdy Mephisto boots and a pair of velvet flats. Striding confidently to the restaurant in a pair of leopard stockings and four-inch Manolo Blahniks, Kempner, who was then sixty-eight and suffering from emphysema, looked down at my flats and said, "They're so . . . sensible." I explained about my knee injury. Not to be outdone, Kempner said that she'd recently broken her hip trying to get into a pair of John Galliano pants. "I just fell over," she said, "and *crack!*" She picked up the pace, and we were practically running down the cobblestone streets to the restaurant. She was way ahead of me, not only in speed but also in her ability to make her feet obey the punitive rules of fashion.

⁂

The World of Gucci has its rules, and I broke a big one. Nobody told me the Gucci event was black-tie. I'd packed a pair of black silk pants and a dressy blouse, which I trusted would be appropriate, but Lee didn't pack a tuxedo, because he routinely doesn't travel with one. "At least I have my Gucci wedding loafers," he said.

Finally, he had another "special event" worthy of them, and he thought the Gucci people would be impressed.

They were not. Our relatively informal attire created a minor ca-tastrophe for the young Gucci PR woman who was assigned to look after me. I'd been seated at a prime table next to actress Evan Rachel Wood, the face of Gucci's perfume Guilty. As it turned out, someone switched the place cards, so I was actually next to Wood's makeup artist, who explained in great detail how she created Evan's various "looks," including her current one, with its focus on a "smoky eye." All Wood wanted to do was meet Madonna, whose face appeared to be in soft focus, as if shrouded in a mist of Gucci perfume. Across from me was James Franco's manager, who announced that Franco, the face of Gucci Pour Homme, wanted to star in a movie about Robert Mapplethorpe and had I ever heard of the photographer?

Really, I could have worn sneakers and a potato sack and no one would have noticed, but at the time it was a Fashion Emergency.

We were at the Peggy Guggenheim Collection when we received the first of a steady stream of e-mails from the Gucci PR woman. She needed my husband's suit size. We were inside the Church of Santa Maria della Salute when my cell phone rang. She wanted to know what I was wearing. I told her. Long pause. "Do you have jewelry?" she asked. Ultimately, I was allowed to wear my own clothes, but the PR woman sent Lee to the San Marco store, where he was fitted into a black suit he had to return the next morning. The suit broadened his shoulders, sucked in his waist, and lengthened his legs. It was like full-length Spanx. I couldn't believe how good he looked. Neither could he. "What about your shoes?" the PR woman wanted to know. He told her the whole Gucci wedding saga while she checked her e-mail. "They're vintage," I added.

I'd packed a pair of four-year-old Louboutin kitten heels that I'd purchased at the Madison Avenue boutique at great cost to my wallet and pride. To ask for anything but the highest heel is to invoke pitying looks from other customers, who know you are not "one of them" and by right shouldn't be allowed in the store. I was happy that at least the salesman allowed me to buy the shoes and didn't tell me they were "training heels" for little girls with big feet. Though I used to love them, next to the Gucci Amazons in stilettos, I felt like Tiny Alice.

With the party only a few hours away, I tried on my outfit and hated the way the pants looked with my unfashionably low heels. I needed a new pair and told Lee I was off to do more sightseeing. Taking the hotel's water taxi from the Giudecca to St. Mark's Square, I began a desperate search for moderate two-inch heels. I believed that extra inch would make all the difference. I couldn't go back into Gucci because I'd already spurned their offer to dress me, so after running from store to store, I wound up in Fendi. I bought the lowest heel I could find—nearly four inches. "Not high at all," said the twentysomething saleswoman. An American tourist, who was also shopping for shoes, looked down at my heels and said, "I love those! I wish I could buy them, but I wouldn't be able to walk."

"You just have to practice," I said. "Then it's easy." The shoe demon had possessed me. Not only was I buying shoes I couldn't walk in, but I was also lying to total strangers about it.

With all the excitement of wearing his new suit, I hoped Lee wouldn't notice my new shoes, but of course he did because I suddenly grew four inches taller, which made me six feet two.

"What do you have on your feet?" he asked.

"Shoes."

"I know they're shoes. But they look new. You didn't just buy them, did you?"

I couldn't lie twice, so I told him the truth.

"You're not going to be able to walk in those things," he said.

"You sound like a broken record."

"Remember Carolyne the Rat."

"Carolyne the Rat had pointy toes," I explained. "These are peep-toe."

"You're still not going to be able to walk in them."

All I needed to do was walk from my hotel to the party at the Cipriani, which is the equivalent of two New York City blocks. If Venetian courtesans could walk the cobbled streets in chopines, I could manage that.

I couldn't. It was torture.

Up ahead, I saw Salma Hayek climbing out of a Gucci speedboat. Her husband, François Pinault owns the company that owns Gucci. I saw Gucci's former designer, Frida Giannini. I saw Robin Wright. I saw Jessica Chastain. I saw Madonna. They were all extremely tall, even Selma Hayek, who in the real world is extremely short, but this wasn't the real world. It was the World of the Few, the Happy Few, the Band of High-Heeled Sisters, and I was determined to be in their company, even if my feet revolted, even if I limped and hobbled, even if I didn't reach my goal . . . *until St. Crispin's Day!*

15

A Pain in the Heel

When Emily was pregnant, my mother wanted to give her my baby shoes. She'd been keeping them for the right occasion and this seemed as good as any. "But they're mine," I said. My mother couldn't understand why I'd want my baby shoes when I was no longer a baby, unless of course I was having a baby. At fifty-one.

I was amazed my mother had even kept the shoes. She'd always hated clutter and as she grew older, she'd toss out anything she could lift without getting a hernia. "What happened to Emily's baby shoes?" I asked. "Why does she need mine?"

"I think I threw hers out," she admitted. "Anyway, all baby shoes look alike."

I explained that for sentimental reasons, I wanted to keep them. I took my first steps in them. I learned how to walk in them. They started me on the journey that led me to where I am now.

"And where is that?" my mother asked.

"In New York, as a writer."

"Too bad the shoes didn't lead you to Oprah. You would have been good on that show."

Since I'd grown up across the street from Jay Leno, my mother had totally unrealistic expectations about celebrity. She thought being famous was easy and failed to understand why I'd yet to achieve that goal, especially since I lived in New York, where celebrities were a dime a dozen.

"Maybe if you'd cast my baby shoes in bronze I could have clobbered someone in the head with them," I said, "and then I'd be known as the Baby Shoe Killer."

"That's not even funny," my mother said. "I bet you haven't thought of your baby shoes in years."

Actually, I'd thought of them just the other day. I was at the nail salon for my semiannual torture session, when the technician started to shave the corn on my baby toe. "Wait," I nearly screamed. "It used to be an extra toe!"

"Oh, that means good luck," she said. I was so deeply touched I agreed to have the Special Spa Pedicure, which cost an extra $40 and involved more pummeling and pounding than any person could possibly endure.

As for my baby shoes, I was fairly sure my sister didn't even want them. I'd seen her only once during her pregnancy, when I'd invited her to the Broadway rock musical *Rent*. She looked beautiful that night, fresh and glowing and happy. Though she'd purposely kept her distance from me, perhaps fearing that if I didn't have a baby, she might not be able to have one either, I was thrilled she was pregnant and hoped it would signal a new beginning. But even today, I can't listen to the show's opening number, "Seasons of Love," without feeling unbearably sad. Jonathan Larson, *Rent*'s thirty-five-year-old creator, died suddenly on the day of the first preview. The song addresses the fleeting nature of time, reducing a year to *"five hundred twenty-five thousand six hundred minutes."*

When Emily gave birth to an adorable little girl, I was overjoyed. I imagined the two of us walking the baby in Central Park. I imagined taking my niece to the theater, museums, and the ballet, showing her the New York I'd grown to love. Maybe I'd even write the children's cat book my mother was always pestering me about. I'd name the main cat after my niece, who would get involved in all sorts of magical adventures. But even though my sister and I live twelve blocks apart, I rarely had the opportunity to see the new baby. I'd try to set up specific times, but they were never convenient. When I did arrange a date, Emily would tell me to call before I came. I'd call and the baby was sleeping. I'd call again and receive the same or a different response, but either way, the message was that if I wanted to see my niece, I had to play by my sister's rules, which to me were increasingly mystifying.

In *A Room of One's Own*, Virgina Woolf, who had a turbulent relationship with her sister, Vanessa Bell, wrote that women are always "thinking back" through their mothers. I'd add that we're also "thinking back" through our sisters, examining our past through our shared history of love and hate, intimacy and rivalry. Because we speak the same "sister tongue" and can encapsulate whole decades of our lives with a grimace or catchphrase, we enjoy a relationship that's far deeper than most. When it's good, it's wonderful, but when it's not, there are few things more painful.

With sisters, you always remember the smallest details, even the ones they wished you'd forget. I remember when Emily sucked her fingers at night, insisting they tasted of butterscotch. I remember the squeaky bed. I remember her crush on Adam West, the original Bat-

man, and on her ninth-grade English teacher. I especially remember
my decapitated doll, Betty.

Over the years, the struggle to reunite Betty played out in different ways. I became a writer, fulfilling my destiny as "Betty's head."
When I didn't get pregnant, I was disappointed but not devastated.
I was hard at work on a book. Emily, who is long-limbed and physically fit, was elated when she became pregnant. When I called to
congratulate her, she cut me off, explaining that it was a private matter between her and her husband. I hung up the phone feeling as if
she'd punched me in the stomach. She subsequently didn't return my
calls. When she finally emerged two weeks later, I was hurt and
confused. "Why didn't you call back?" I asked. Drawing on a lifetime
of pent-up emotion, she lashed out. "It's always about you, isn't it?"
Then she added, "You don't know what it means to be a sister!"

Being a sister was an integral part of my identity, and over the
years, I'd considered myself a good one. I'd always been there for
Emily and couldn't fathom how she could actually say that I didn't
know what it meant to be a sister. It seemed cruel and unnecessary.
It also seemed totally wrong.

My mother, who had only one brother, had always been desperate
for sisters, imagining a warm, wonderful *Little Women* scenario. She
expected us to be the March girls, though if she'd looked deeper into
Louisa May Alcott's life, she would have found complications there
too. "You were always so happy together," she'd say, which was not
entirely true. With three children, sibling relationships are often tri-
angulated, and at different points of their lives, one usually feels left
out. There were times when Emily was close to Nancy, other times
when she was closer to me. It was just the way it went.

Once Emily got married and had a baby, however, she had her
own family, which seemed to preclude her old one. It was as if the

two universes couldn't intersect. Before her wedding, when she moved out of my old apartment, she made a point of telling me that she'd left a coat behind. It happened to be one that Lee and I had given her. That said everything. She no longer needed or wanted my protection; she would soon have a husband to fill that role. I'd become dispensable, like the coat. Since that wasn't something she could articulate to my mother—indeed, she may not have even been aware of it—she needed reasons not to talk to me and continually found them.

After we planned a vacation at the end of August that happened to coincide with my niece's first birthday, Emily expected me to cancel the trip. When I told her it wasn't possible due to Lee's work schedule and suggested we celebrate the following weekend, she didn't speak to me for a year. *Five hundred twenty-five thousand six hundred minutes.*

There were countless incidents in which I continually did something "wrong," which gave her the freedom to stay mad so she didn't have to actually see me. When I dropped off a present for my niece one Christmas, Emily returned the gift with a note saying that I owed her the gift of an apology. It involved something a friend's daughter had said to my niece the previous Christmas. The daughter apologized the next day, and in any event, it had nothing to do with me. Still, I persisted in trying to fix things without knowing what was broken. I invited Emily to the opera, but she never wanted to go. I continued to send my niece birthday and Christmas presents, receiving polite but curt thank-you notes in return.

One day, I passed Emily on the opposite side of Madison Avenue. She was with my niece, who was then five or six, and a handful of mothers from her daughter's school. I was coming from the radiologist's office after my yearly mammogram. Though our mother didn't have breast cancer until she was sixty-four, I—we—have always been categorized as being at high risk, and I'm always a nervous wreck before my checkups. But luckily, everything was fine and I felt like buying something to celebrate.

"Hey, I'm okay," I wanted to tell my sister as she walked toward me. "They didn't find anything!" I pictured us going shoe shopping together and then sitting at an outdoor café, where we'd laugh so much that the women at the next table, noting our similar voices and blue eyes, would whisper enviably, "Oh, they must be sisters!" But we didn't go shopping or have lunch or laugh. We didn't even say hello. Instead, we hid behind our sunglasses, passing each other as if we were strangers and continued to walk in opposite directions.

Finally, my mother, who is nothing if not persistent, convinced Emily to invite us to see her daughter dance in *The Nutcracker*. For the next several years, the only time I saw my niece was when she was in ballet slippers onstage. At that rate, I figured the only way I'd ever get to know her was through all the various roles, up to and beyond Sugar Plum Fairy.

My mother couldn't understand why her daughters were "fighting." She kept pushing me to make contact, once going so far as to convince me to call Emily on my own birthday. I felt ridiculous, and it didn't matter anyway. Emily remained elusive. She never showed up at Thanksgiving because Nancy and I were there, visiting my parents when she knew we'd be absent. Perhaps as a middle child it was the only way she could carve out a unique identity for herself. I'd always run interference between Emily and Nancy, acting as a mediator during their frequent misunderstandings, but now that Emily and I were no longer close, the sibling ecosystem was thrown off balance. When Nancy became pregnant with her daughter Isabel, she assumed it would bring her closer to Emily, and I feared I'd be the one left behind. On more than one occasion, Emily had told me pointedly that a "book is not a child," but Emily and Nancy didn't bond over their children; in fact, by having a baby, Nancy had introduced another "Betty" into the family dynamic, and Emily didn't want to hear about her.

I desperately wanted to fix the situation, because that was my designated family role, but no matter what I did, nothing worked. I discussed it so much with my therapist that even she was growing frustrated. Whenever I uttered the word *sisters* to my friends, I saw a look in their eyes that said, *Please, not again*! Finally, I told myself, "Enough!" Whenever my mother brought up the subject, which she did frequently, I begged her to let it go. "Emily is happy," I explained. "She has a wonderful husband and a smart, talented daughter. Maybe she needed to cut ties so she could be her own person. Let it be."

I hoped my mother would catch the Beatles reference, but she was having none of it. She prayed for reconciliation, and finally, her prayers were answered, when all of her daughters developed plantar fasciitis, the most common cause of heel pain. It happens when the thick band of tissue—the plantar fascia—that runs from the bottom of your foot to your toes becomes inflamed, due to a number of reasons, including overuse or improper footwear. "Improper" means flats *and* high heels, so I could no longer be self-righteous about wearing sensible shoes.

"You should talk to Emily about this," my mother said. "She went through the same thing!" My mother was practically giddy at the notion that we might bond over our mutual sore heels. I suspect she'd have been even happier if Emily had needed an organ transplant, figuring that if I gave her one of my kidneys, she'd be obligated to call now and then.

I commiserated with Nancy, who gave me the same advice she always gives:

"You should see my chiropractor. He's incredible." Since her chiropractor lives in Boston, it wasn't the most practical recommendation. She then suggested ice and rest, neither of which she'd bothered with due to her extremely high tolerance for pain. Years ago, she taught aerobics, and her class was so difficult she received hate mail, and yet everyone kept coming back for more.

"Don't worry about it," she said. "It will go away."

"Has yours?"

"No, but I've blocked it out."

I decided to go to the podiatrist I'd seen once before. He plays flamenco guitar, which I didn't know at the time so was left wondering why a podiatrist would have three very long glossy nails on his right hand. He must have seen me staring because he immediately explained about his guitar playing, though he probably would have done so anyway. In my experience, foot doctors seem to be unduly proud of their hobbies. I remembered my fencing podiatrist and his recommendation for my overpronation. I doubted flamenco guitar would do much for heel pain.

I made a point of wearing tie shoes with special "revolutionary" air insoles. He squeezed them between his fingers before rolling them up in a ball. "These are useless," he said. "No support."

He wanted to know how long I'd had the pain and I told him about two years. "You've been walking around in pain for two years and never thought of doing anything about it?" he asked.

I explained that at first it was a dull ache that didn't really bother me until the pain grew intense. I blamed Vera Wang. We met in her office so I could interview her for a story, and she had on Martin Margiela's split-toed stacked-heeled Tabi boots. I didn't like the boots but admired Wang's attitude. Every word out of her mouth was "fierce," and for someone in her sixties, she was definitely that. I looked down at her chic, if slightly ridiculous, boots and then at my boring flat boots, and I realized I needed fierce. After the interview, I walked thirteen blocks to Saks, where I barely managed to reach their 10022-Shoe Salon, before I had to sit down on a banquette. The dull ache in my heel was now throbbing like mad.

After the podiatrist performed a sonogram, he told me that I had a slight tear in the fascia of my right foot and a barely imperceptible one in my left. He told me to stop walking for exercise. He told me ideally that I should stop walking entirely, but since that wasn't possible, he told me to wear supportive sneakers. Reluctantly, I followed his advice, but my heel pain kept getting worse, especially in the mornings. He then gave me a CAM Walker boot, a strap-on orthopedic device that controls and stabilizes the foot in order to promote healing. The boot lasted a week. It threw off my normal gait and gave me lower back pain, which for a writer is worse than heel pain. On my return appointment, I knew by the look in the podiatrist's eyes that I'd become a Problem Patient. His office walls were filled with glowing autographed testimonials from major ballet stars and sports figures. He'd fixed their valuable feet, but somehow my foot, which didn't need to plié or pirouette or do anything more strenuous than walk at a brisk pace around Central Park, refused to cooperate. He sent me for an MRI of my foot to rule out any fractures. I had none. He said we could try "platelet-rich plasma therapy," which involved injecting my own blood into my foot, but that sounded too weird, so his last and final suggestion was to buy a pair of MBTs.

MBT stands for Masai Barefoot Technology. The Masai, a semi-nomadic tribe from East Africa, are famous for their excellent posture, athletic ability, and freedom from joint pain. A Swiss engineer named Karl Müller discovered their secret: walking barefoot on soft sand and grass. MBTs, with their curved "rocker" soles, were designed to mimic that effect. Even though they sounded like a modern variant of Earth shoes, I bought them, wearing them for several weeks without any relief. And then I began to wonder if the Masai didn't complain of joint pain because they had bigger things to complain about, such as lack of food and water. Then I saw pictures of Masai men wearing sandals made of tire rubber, so by that point I was totally confused. Out went the MBTs.

⚜

After a year, the pain in my right heel went away—and migrated to my left heel. Discouraged, I dumped all the shoes I'd probably never wear again into a canvas bag and brought them to a consignment shop. I hoped to recoup some of the money I'd foolishly spent on them. The shop, on the second floor, was packed with designer merchandise. We were then in the midst of the financial crisis and women were emptying their closets, which meant the owner could be extremely picky. I lined up behind a woman with a stack of Chanel suits, some still bearing the original price tags. The tyrannical owner stood behind a glass case, where they kept their most precious items, such as Hermès Birkin bags that cost even more than at the Hermès boutique.

After the woman carefully inspected the Chanel items, rejecting one because it had a tiny stain, she turned to my shoes. By then, there was a long line of women behind me.

"Our customers don't like these," she said, referring to a pair of Roger Vivier buckled pumps. "Our customers like Louboutin, Manolo, and maybe Jimmy Choo."

"These are iconic shoes," I said about the pumps. "Catherine Deneuve wore them in Buñuel's *Belle de Jour.*"

"I'm not here to argue with you," she said, shoving them back at me. "What else do you have?"

I dipped into my canvas bag, pulling out my Carolynes. She looked at them as if inspecting cancer cells under a microscope.

"No, too old," she said.

"But they're classics."

"To some people, but not to our customers."

She agreed to take a pair of Manolo Blahnik python pumps, which I'd bought new at the same consignment shop, along with Manolo flats that I purchased right before I developed my plantar fasciitis. They were pristine. The line of consignees was getting longer, the woman behind the glass case more impatient. Luckily, I'd saved the best for last: two pairs of Louboutin ankle boots, newly polished and soled.

"No," the woman said.

"*No?* They're Louboutins."

"But they have black soles," she said.

"Yes, I just redid them."

"That was a big mistake. Our customers want the red soles."

"Wait a minute," I said. "Are you saying that you won't take perfectly good Louboutin boots because the soles aren't red?"

"That's exactly what I'm saying. . . . *Next.*"

The woman behind me offered a piece of advice: "Take them to Leather Spa in midtown. They resole Louboutins with red rubber that's the exact same shade."

Another woman followed me as I headed downstairs. "What size are the Louboutins?" she whispered. After I told her, she said, "Meet me at the cash machine on the corner of Madison and 79th Street, and we can strike a deal." I thanked her but said no. I imagined being arrested for selling counterfeit goods because even the New York police probably knew that Louboutins had red soles.

꙯

A few weeks later, I ran into Emily on Madison Avenue, not far from where her daughter attends school. I hadn't seen my niece since she was a *Nutcracker* angel, but I kept the conversation upbeat and cordial, following my mother's advice to seek advice about my sore heel. Since she and her daughter were walking home and I was doing an errand not far from where she lived, I said, "I'll walk with you." It was clear she wasn't thrilled, but not wanting to risk a heel flair-up by running away, she agreed. "Do you have any ideas about what to wear?" I asked. She suggested the Arche shoes, which are made with natural latex that helps with shock absorption. She was wearing a cute pair of Arche ankle boots in teal. While I wear mostly dark colors, she tends to gravitate toward colorful ones.

We continued to walk down Madison, having a perfectly pleasant if slightly strained conversation about our feet, when she suddenly said, "Well, I'm going this way." She'd obviously had enough "sister time" for one afternoon. "Oh, okay," I said. "I guess I'll see you, then."

I decided to walk to the Arche store, where I told the saleswoman my sister had recommended it. "We both have plantar fasciitis," I said, as if to make up for what we didn't have, which was a relationship. "What does you sister look like?" she asked. I described her as a tall blonde with size 8½ feet.

"I think I remember her," she said. "Does she have a daughter?"

"Yeah, my niece."

"Oh, that's nice," she added. "You must have a lot of fun together."

"Yes, lots."

The saleswoman looked at my feet and shook her head. "You're very narrow. Our shoes run wide. But let me see what I have." She returned with a pair of lace-up boots that looked like something Heidi might wear to herd sheep in the Alps.

"They also come in a pretty shade of teal," she said.

"No, I can't wear teal. That's my sister's color."

Since they were the only ones that ran narrow, I bought them—in black. When I called my mother later that night, I told her about running into Emily, even though I knew I was opening up Pandora's box.

"I'm so happy you're finally talking again," she said.

"I wouldn't say we were exactly talking. She just told me where to get shoes."

"I think that's very encouraging. Telling someone where to get shoes is like . . ."

"Telling someone where to get shoes."

"Well, that's something."

☙

With my heel still inflamed, I made an appointment with a doctor known around town as "the rock star of podiatrists." Waiting in his office, I sat next to a fashionably dressed woman who was back for a follow-up appointment. She was wearing four-inch heeled sandals. Maybe the doctor was a miracle worker after all. He started off by telling me I needed another sonogram because he didn't trust the other podiatrist's equipment. After I had the sonogram, the doctor gave me the good news. I didn't need physical therapy or a CAM boot or even orthopedic shoes. What I needed were orthotics, and I didn't just need one pair, I needed three—for sneakers, flats, and heels. They were inscribed with his name, so now I had designer orthotics that cost $2,500, which my health insurance actually covered.

Several days later, I received a note from the consignment shop; after three months and several markdowns, nobody had purchased my Blahnik flats. I had two choices: They could donate them to charity, or I could pick them up. Since they were brand-new and perhaps wearable, thanks to my rock star inserts, I went down to the shop and reclaimed them. The soles were all scuffed and the leather wrinkled.

"Excuse me," I said to the woman behind the glass case, "but who's been walking in my shoes?"

"The shoes have been here for three months," she informed me. "Lots of people have tried them on."

"Did you let them walk up and down the street? These were brand-new."

"I'm sorry you're upset that your shoes didn't sell. We have a very discerning clientele. . . . *Next.*"

I wore my rock star inserts everywhere. Since I was now wary of both flats and heels, I settled on a pair of suede loafers with an elevated heel from a company named Thierry Rabotin. They were extremely comfortable and my orthotics fit nicely inside them, and who cared if I saw a ninety-year-old woman in the same ones? My heel still ached, but I figured it would take time.

"Time isn't on your side," my mother said. "Call your sister. I think she went to a physical therapist. Get the name from her."

"Mom, I just went to one of the best foot doctors in New York, and he said I didn't need physical therapy."

"You know what's coming up? *The Nutcracker.*"

"Believe it or not, I don't keep track of time based on *The Nut-cracker*."

"I hope you're going."

"I'm supposed to invite myself to *The Nutcracker* and just show up?"

"Patricia, I'm old. You don't know how long I have to live. I could go tomorrow."

"You're going to be around forever, Mom."

"You don't know that. Please, do this for me. Call your sister, get a recommendation for a therapist, and then go to *The Nutcracker*."

I called my sister, who gave me the name of her therapist, telling me she didn't think he was very good. With that ringing endorsement, I made an appointment with him. After I filled out all the paperwork, I informed him that he'd treated my sister for the same condition. In fact, my sister in Boston also had plantar fasciitis. I thought he'd find this so fascinating he'd immediately want to do a research study on the genetic component of plantar fasciitis in female siblings, but he was more interested in watching the football game on ESPN. After icing my foot, the therapist used a TENS machine, applying sensors attached to electrodes as part of a protocol to stimulate the nerves. He explained that I'd get the best results from the highest intensity. Starting at the lowest level, he kept increasing the voltage, until we reached a point where I could barely tolerate it. He left it on for fifteen minutes while I practiced deep breathing to distract myself from the zapping pain.

"How's it going?" he asked in between watching football plays.

"Okay, but it's starting to hurt."

He checked back a few minutes later. "Can you handle the pain?"

"I'm not sure."

"Give it a few more minutes."

"Okay, take it off," I practically screamed. "It's unbearable."

When he unhooked the sensors, I heard him say, "Oops!" I figured he'd mistakenly put it on the highest level, but he'd actually forgotten to turn the machine on.

Embarrassed, I joked about the power of the mind, but in his eyes I saw Problem Patient. I went for six more treatments, none of which were successful even with the machine on, and finally the therapist said he couldn't help me. When I left, I heard him say to his supervisor, "I'm not sure it's plantar fasciitis. All her sisters have it. I think it's a psychological problem."

⚘

Lee and I went to *The Nutcracker*, where my niece danced the role of Party Girl. She was all grown up and wearing toe shoes. Lee asked if perhaps they'd like to go out and get some ice cream, but Emily explained it was a school night. We walked with them to a corner to share a cab and then dropped them off at their apartment.

The next day, my mother said my niece had caught a chill because we walked too far to get the cab. My sister apparently had wanted to hail one in front of the theater.

"So now I gave her a cold?"

"I just don't want to die without the two of you speaking."

"I'm speaking. There's just no one to speak to."

"Patricia, are you aware of how fast the years go by?"

Five hundred twenty-five thousand six hundred minutes . . .

16

Feetfirst

The white squirrels arrived in my parents' backyard about seven years ago. I'd never seen white squirrels before and viewed them as good luck charms. As long as they remained nearby, I clung to the childish belief that they'd keep my white-haired parents safe from harm.

My parents were then in their mid-eighties with the normal share of age-related health problems. Ten years earlier, my father had had a sextuple bypass. He and my mother had been visiting us for Christmas, and as we walked around Greenwich Village, I noticed him lagging behind. With my sisters and mother up ahead, I kept pace with him. "Are you feeling okay?" I asked. He answered, as he always did, "I'm fine." But it was clear that the man who prided himself on "never falling out of a march" was having a hard time simply walking down the street. I insisted my mother call the doctor the minute they got home, and after my father had an angiogram, he was taken immediately to the hospital for surgery.

From then on, I was on tenterhooks. No Morrisroe male relative had ever made it past seventy-nine. He was then seventy-eight. But after a period of adjustment and denial—my father insisted the doctor misdiagnosed him—he resumed his life, even traveling overseas with my mother. All was fine until Nancy's wedding five years later. Prior to the rehearsal dinner, my mother decided that my father didn't have the right shoes and wanted him to rush out and buy a new pair. In addition to all the pressure and excitement of the wedding, I suspect the shoe problem may have caused his blood pressure to rise. Or perhaps it was just a coincidence. In any event, when he appeared at the dinner, I knew something was wrong and kept asking him if he was okay. Naturally, he kept telling me he was fine. The next morning it was evident to me that he'd suffered a mild stroke, but at the time I didn't realize the importance of acting quickly when symptoms appear. I just knew that if I took him to the hospital, Nancy would call off the wedding and my father would never forgive himself for ruining the day. When my father saw Nancy in her wedding gown at the church, he was beaming. "You look beautiful," he said, but he had a hard time pronouncing the words. At this point I was a total wreck. I kept a close watch on him the whole time, but my father not only walked Nancy down the aisle but also managed to dance with her to "Daddy's Little Girl."

The next morning, Lee and I took him to the emergency ward, where tests showed that indeed he'd suffered a stroke. "All because of the shoes," my mother said. She felt terrible about getting him upset. He felt terrible that he'd ruined Nancy's wedding. (In truth, very few people even noticed.) I was amazed at his strength and resolve. He didn't fall out of a march even after a stroke. Though he took the prescribed medication, he refused any occupational or physical therapy and eventually recovered on his own.

In terms of his everyday functioning, my father's biggest issue was his progressive hearing loss. Though he wore hearing aids, they didn't seem to offer much help, resulting in increased isolation. He stopped going to social functions, and it was painful to watch him struggle to keep pace with family conversations. As time went on, he retreated more and more into his reading.

In the mid-1990s, my mother had been diagnosed with atrial fibrillation, an abnormal heart rhythm that could possibly lead to stroke. She also had essential tremor, a neurological disorder that causes rhythmic shaking. After I told her that Katharine Hepburn had suffered from the same condition, she felt a little better but still hated what she called her "shaky, shake, shakes."

In 2007, we bought a small weekend house, which my mother wanted to see, but she couldn't leave my father alone. In a reversal of roles, she was physically stronger than he was, though you wouldn't have known it judging by appearance. She looked as if a gust of wind could have blown her away, which is exactly what happened when she was nine years old and living in North Andover. She told the story often. Walking across an endless field, the wind howling like banshees, she felt herself being tossed "for miles" like tumbleweed, until she landed on a frozen lake. She broke her arm, the zigzag scar still visible after eight decades. A neighborhood boy discovered her and carried her home.

I found the tale so dramatic that I would forever associate my mother with tumbleweed. She'd always struck me as someone who might easily take flight, a victim of the elements, but I was wrong. She was definitely flighty, but despite her fragile appearance, she was extremely sturdy, with boundless energy that was all the more remarkable given her advanced age. Whenever my mother would describe her week, I couldn't believe she could handle such a packed and grueling schedule. There were countless doctors' appointments encompassing every specialty—cardiology, urology, dermatology, ophthalmology, gynecology, podiatry, nephrology, and so on.

Her one pleasurable appointment was her weekly wash and set, which she never missed, even in snowstorms. Mrs. Godfrey had died years earlier, so she went to another salon in the center of town. When it moved to North Andover, my mother moved with it. Most days, after my parents had lunch together, and if they didn't have doctors' appointments, my mother would jump into the car and drive to Kohl's or Home Goods. She loved driving, and she loved buying things. She especially loved returning the things she bought. It was all part of the rhythm of her life. When she tripped over the vacuum cord and broke her wrist, she still kept driving while wearing a cast. She hated the idea of being housebound.

Remarkably, my mother maintained her frenetic schedule on very little sleep. We both suffered from insomnia and when I wrote a book about it, I thought she might be interested, but after reading the first few chapters, she decided it wasn't for her. "I don't think it's anybody's business that I have insomnia," she told me. "And I'm very upset that you described Sister Margaret as having meaty hands."

"She's probably dead now, so what does it matter? And she did have meaty hands. Plus, she was mean."

"You'll never get on *Oprah* now," she told me. "She's not Catholic, but she's very spiritual."

"Okay, but did you get beyond the nun part and read anything about sleep science?"

"No, I was too upset about Sister Margaret. And just wait until your father reads it. He's going to have *plenty* to say."

"Maybe he can say it on *Oprah*."

"You're very fresh."

And so it went.

✧

One year when Lee and I went home for Thanksgiving, I looked for the white squirrels, but they were gone.

"Where are they?" I asked my mother.

"What are you talking about?"

"The white squirrels."

"You mean those pests?"

It soon became clear that my mother didn't share my feelings about the white squirrels and in fact wanted them dead. She kept a bird feeder outside the kitchen window, and the squirrels climbed up the pole and ate the seeds. My mother began greasing the pole with cooking oil so they'd slide off. I'd be on the phone with her and she'd say, "One of the squirrels nearly broke its neck. That's what you get for stealing birdseed." I begged her not to kill the squirrels, "because they represent you and Daddy."

"You think we're like squirrels? Thanks a lot, Patricia." Then she thought for a second. "*Squirrels!* What about a children's book about two white-haired squirrels."

"I don't want to write a children's book."

My mother began rapping on the kitchen window. "*Get away from that bird feeder or I'll take a potshot at both of you!*"

"You've got a gun?"

"Of course I don't have a gun, but if I did, they'd be in big trouble."

"That's a great ending for a children's story," I said. "The grand-mother kills the squirrels."

"In *Little Red Riding Hood,* the wolf eats the grandmother, and that didn't prevent the story from becoming a classic. It's too bad you missed your true calling."

"As a children's book writer?"

"Or a real estate lawyer. Your father thought you'd be very good at it. You should have listened to him. If you had, we'd all be out in the Hamptons right now enjoying Thanksgiving without the squirrels."

My mother loved holidays. For Halloween, she'd tie corn husks around the lamppost, carve pumpkins, and buy a ton of candy for the trick-or-treaters, eating all the leftovers until it made her sick. Valentine's Day meant more candy, along with hearts and flowers and cards. Christmas wasn't Christmas without a tree, and it couldn't be a fake one, it had to be a Fraser fir. Even when she could barely walk, she'd somehow manage to get a sizable one into her car and then wrangle a neighbor to help her stick it in the tree stand. Nancy, who is allergic to tree sap, was called upon to hang the ornaments, which she did wearing elbow-length latex gloves. Throughout my childhood, my mother had always created such a festive holiday atmosphere that I continued to believe in Santa much longer than any of my peers. When she finally told me the truth, I collapsed on the bathroom floor, hysterical. I was twelve.

Of all the holidays, however, Thanksgiving was my mother's favorite. Though she'd never been much of a cook, she always pulled together a fabulous meal, first driving to Raymond's Turkey Farm for a fresh turkey and then, with the help of my father, she'd tie up the "bird" and "wrestle" it into the oven. While the turkey roasted, she'd make her famous party potatoes, which in her Boston accent she pronounced "pahty badaydoes." She combined mashed potatoes with a stick of butter and a container of cream cheese, sprinkling paprika on top. One serving amounted to my daily caloric intake. My father always said grace, thanking God for bringing the family together, but for the past ten years, Emily and her family were absent.

In 2013, when my mother was ninety-two and her "shaky, shake, shakes" were worsening, she still insisted on cooking Thanksgiving dinner. Nancy drove her to Raymond's to buy the turkey, but my mother and father still managed to get it in the oven on their own. After we finished the meal and did the dishes, my mother asked me to follow her upstairs to her bedroom. She plopped down on the edge of the bed, "pooped" from all the preparations, and then had me open the bottom drawer of her bureau. Nestled beneath her mother's wedding shawl was a small package wrapped in yellowed tissue paper. I pictured two mummified toes, like E.T.'s index finger. I was repulsed, yet oddly exhilarated. Though I had no idea what I'd do with them, I was touched she'd finally acknowledged their existence. She unwrapped the paper, holding the objects in the palm of her hand.

"These are your baby shoes," my mother said. "I hope you'll make good use of them."

I didn't want to appear ungrateful, especially on Thanksgiving, but I casually mentioned that I'd been hoping for toes. At this point, it had become almost a running gag with us.

"*Toes?* What on earth are you talking about?" my mother said. "Why would I keep toes in a bureau drawer?"

"For good luck?"

"You think toes are like *what*? A rabbit's foot?"

"In parts of Asia, they are."

"We don't live in Asia, Patricia. This toe obsession of yours is totally morbid. You let your imagination run away with you and it certain hasn't helped your career."

"As a writer?"

"As a *children's* book writer. It's a good thing your father doesn't know about all this toe craziness, because he'd have *plenty* to say about it."

I went back downstairs, where my father was in his reading chair staring at the *Eagle-Tribune*. I've rarely asked him a direct question but decided to go for it.

"Did I have twelve toes when I was born?"

He put down the paper. "They weren't toes," he answered readily. "Just tiny pieces of skin. The doctor snipped them off. It was nothing."

"Oh," I said. "So that's it. Just tiny pieces of skin?" The mystery was finally solved.

"But you did have jaundice," he added.

"See," my mother said, catching the end of the conversation. "I told you!"

"I remember distinctly that you once said I had twelve toes," I persisted. "It was on the day the police shot the skunk."

"The police shot a skunk? Patricia, really!"

"About the twelve toes . . ."

"Okay, well, maybe I did say that, but then I took it back."

"Why?"

"Because I didn't want you to think you weren't a perfect baby."

⚝

The next evening, Lee, my mother, and I were watching TV in the den, which used to be Bumpa's bedroom. One of the channels was showing a special on 1960s pop music, and my mother started singing along with vintage footage of Herman's Hermits. *"I'm 'Enry the Eighth, I am, 'Enry the Eighth, I am, I am."* Lee looked over at me, as if to say, *How in the world does she know that?*

"I wish they'd show the Beatles," my mother said. "Paul was my favorite."

"I remember."

We were both sitting on the couch, her legs stretched over my lap.

"I have bad arthritis in my feet," she said. "They hurt a lot, and they're stiff as boards. They're practically useless." She wiggled her toes.

"Do you remember Bumpa's foot rubs?" she asked. "He had healing hands."

"Would you like a little foot rub?" I asked.

We listened to the Dave Clark Five and Petula Clark and the Byrds while I massaged her tired, worn-out feet. "It's just like the old days, isn't it?" she said. "I miss them."

✿

My mother needed new sneakers, so the following day, Lee and I took her to the New Balance factory outlet, which is in Lawrence, across from the former textile mills. The "Big Ben" tower clock that had stopped running in the 1950s was restored in the 1990s and now keeps accurate time. New Balance claims to be one of the few companies committed to the domestic shoe business, but more and more of its products are being manufactured in Asia. My mother didn't care where they were made; she only cared that New Balance would restore her old balance.

"If I can only find the right pair, I know I'll be fine," she told me. I didn't have the heart to tell her that sneakers wouldn't correct her balance or reset the clock. The parking lot was on a steep incline, so Lee dropped us off while he parked the car. After we helped her into the store, we found the 8½ medium section. Since it was a factory outlet, we had to fend for ourselves. My mother sat down on a bench, while I pulled out various models, which she rejected for multiple reasons. "I am not a teenager, Patricia," she said. "Can you imagine me in orange? Or lime? No, I want something subdued."

"Like gray?" I asked.

"Gray? Ugh! Too depressing. I'm not in the grave yet."

"I have the same pair, and I like them."

"You have your father's feet. Very narrow."

"But these come in medium."

She turned up her nose. "I don't like gray."

I found another pair, gray and pale blue. "What do you think?" I asked. At this point, Lee had disappeared into the men's department. He is the most patient man I have ever met, but even he has his limits.

My mother made a face. I convinced her to try them on. They were too big. She tried on a smaller pair. They were too small. We tried on at least six different pairs in various sizes, colors, and styles. Finally, she found a pair she liked. I suggested that she walk in them to make sure they fit properly. "I am not using my cane," she said defiantly. "Remember, I used to go to Silver Sneakers." She was referring to an exercise program for older adults that she'd attended fifteen years earlier. I helped her walk up and down the aisle. She was pretty sure they fit. I was worried about the "pretty sure" part, but we'd already gone through all the sneakers in her size.

"I'm delighted with them," she announced back in the car. "I'm so glad you came with me. I would never be able to do this myself. The incline in the parking lot is treacherous. I'd probably kill myself. But these are perfect. Thank you, Patricia and Lee. Now I won't have to use my cane."

Back in New York, I called my mother. "So, how are the sneakers?"

"I brought them back. They didn't fit, and I didn't like the colors."

"You walked from the parking lot to the store? You said it was treacherous! You said it could kill you!"

"Those sneakers would have killed me. Anyway, you'll be happy to know I bought the gray ones."

I gently suggested that maybe my mother should stop driving and hire someone to help her do the food shopping and errands.

"If I can't drive, that's it for me," she said. "You expect me to be stuck in the house all day long? I'll go crazy. I love getting outside and walking places. Take that away from me, and it's over."

Her favorite destination was Whole Foods, where she worked the system like a pro. First, she parked in the handicapped spot and then got her cane from the backseat and walked to the shopping carts, which were usually in front. Once she steadied herself with a cart, she was all set. There were always "kind" people ready to help, probably because they couldn't believe someone that old and frail was walking around a warehouse-size supermarket on her own. Every day I expected to receive a call from someone at Whole Foods telling me she'd collapsed near the kale chips.

The following September, my mother did indeed fall—not at Whole Foods but nearer to home, more specifically, at the bird feeder. She claimed she was trying to fill it with birdseed, though I suspected she was attempting to grease the pole to keep the white squirrels away. Since my father couldn't hear her cries for help, she crawled the whole length of the backyard to attract his attention. She had to move quickly to avoid the sprinkler system, which was timed to go on. When my father saw her on the ground, he immediately called 911 and an ambulance took her to the local hospital. The doctors couldn't find anything wrong, but given her age—she was about to turn ninety-three—they wanted to keep her overnight for more tests the next morning. Nancy drove from Boston to stay with my father. Around three A.M., my mother decided she'd had enough of the hospital and demanded to be let out. Remarkably, given the liability issues, they actually released her in the middle of the night and an ambulance brought her home. When she got there, she discovered that she didn't have her house keys. My father had removed his hearing aids and Nancy is a heavy sleeper, so nobody heard the doorbell.

My quick-thinking mother convinced the EMS workers to get a ladder from the garage and then climb up to the roof, where they had to remove an air-conditioner to gain entrance through a second-story window. Nancy woke up to find two strange men in the hallway and screamed.

When my mother told me the story, I said, "That's the craziest thing I ever heard. You should have stayed in the hospital."

"I didn't want to be in the hospital. I wanted to be home. The only way they're going to take me out is feetfirst."

We hired a home-care attendant against my parents' strenuous objections. My mother hated having someone else in the house, but it was clear she needed help with errands. She continued to complain that she was tired, but with her insomnia, it was hard to know if she wasn't getting enough sleep or if it was more serious. Though I'd begged her not to do it, she'd renewed her driver's license, but she didn't feel well enough to drive or even accompany the attendant to Whole Foods or to her hairdresser's. The only thing she cared about was Thanksgiving. Emily and her family had promised to come home, and my mother was looking forward to finally seeing everyone together at the table.

Two days before the holiday, she was taken to the emergency ward again, this time with an excruciating headache. Or was it eye pain? It was hard to keep up with the ever-shifting complaints. The doctors at the hospital diagnosed congestive heart disease, and she was sent to a nearby nursing home for rehabilitation. Coincidentally, it was the same place where Priscilla Lane, the movie star and mother of the girl with the white Mary Janes, had spent her final years.

On Thanksgiving, everyone was at the dining room table, except my mother. I sat in her chair, propping up her driver's license against a candlestick so she'd be present in spirit.

The following morning, Lee and I brought my father over to visit her. Since he rarely left his reading chair, it was difficult for him to move, and we were nervous that he'd slip and fall. We helped him to the door of the nursing home, where we'd arranged for a wheelchair. When he saw my mother being wheeled out of her room, his green eyes lit up with such love I had to hold back tears. I'd never seen that expression before, or maybe I'd just never looked hard enough for it. We took them both into a private room, where they sat side by side and held hands. My father kept moving his wheelchair back and forth, as if on a first date and he didn't know what to say.

Back home, my father showed me the blue-and-white Victorian figurine of a little boy that sat on a side table next to the couch. It had been there forever, but I'd never really noticed it. My father explained that before he was sent away to boarding school, the landlady at the rooming house where he lived with his father told him he could select one thing to keep him company. He picked the little boy and somehow managed to hold on to it for the next eighty-five years. "Look over there," he said, pointing to a blue-and-white little girl figurine. Again, it was one of those objects that had always been next to the couch but that I'd never paid any attention to. He told me that when he first met my mother, it was the first thing he noticed in her apartment. The little girl was the perfect match to the little boy.

⁂

My mother spent the next several weeks in the nursing home, trying to regain her strength. She pushed as hard as she could in physical therapy, but she hated the place, complaining that the aides were rough and the food terrible. Once, after an aide yelled at her for pressing the call button too many times, both Nancy and I were on the phone with the social worker and nursing station. Another time an aide upbraided her for not making it to the bathroom on time. It was humiliating for my proud mother, and once again, we spoke to the staff, but it didn't seem to matter. Though we explained that my mother didn't like eggs, they persisted in serving them to her. Deciding that she was dehydrated, they put her on an IV drip and in the process managed to blow a vein, causing blood to leak out. I was the one who noticed that her arm, with its paper-thin skin, was all swollen.

There were a few bright spots. One day she received a bunch of tulips from my friend Robin. Steffi had introduced us right before she'd died, making a point of telling me, "You two should become friends." It was if she'd willed her to me, and we did indeed become close. My mother had always loved flowers, and as the tulips opened up and changed shape, she found them mesmerizing. "These are simply the most beautiful flowers I've ever seen," she told me. "I could watch them for hours."

She spent much of the day sleeping, however, and after she told me she'd had a dream of walking through her childhood home, I began to get nervous. I knew that such dreams are common at the end of life. "Mom, you don't think you're dying, do you?" I asked hesitantly. She immediately turned into her old self. "Patricia, how could you ask such a question? Of course I'm not dying. Really! You always have to make such a big deal out of things."

A few days before Christmas, Lee and I drove to Andover to bring my mother back home. The nurses and social worker gave out very little information on her progress, and the doctor didn't return calls. When we went to see her, one of the attendants called me aside. "I shouldn't be saying this," she whispered. "But you really should get her out of here. She's not improving at all. All she does is sleep."

"We're bringing her home," I explained. "That's why we're here."

It took several days for the paperwork to be processed before my mother could be released, so Lee and I bought a tree and decorated it with all her favorite ornaments.

We hung the mantelpiece decoration Bumpa had made fifty years earlier; he'd cut out little angels, choirboys, and snowmen from pieces of colored felt, gluing sequins for eyes. We put a Christmas wreath on the front door, white poinsettias around the fireplace, and arranged to have the tree in front of the house outlined in white lights. It had snowed recently and, to use one of my mother's favorite expressions, it looked just like "a winter wonderland." My parents were about to celebrate their sixty-fifth wedding anniversary on December 27. It had snowed on that day too, as it had on my wedding, and at Bumpa's funeral, and on the days Nancy and I were born.

The morning we were scheduled to pick her up, we got a call from someone at the nursing home. There was a bad virus going around and my mother had caught it. "You shouldn't come over," the woman said. "It's too contagious."

Lee and I went anyway. I have never seen anyone as sick as my mother. All I could do was hold her. In the hallway, I passed the attendant who'd advised me to get my mother out of the place; she gave me a sympathetic glance and then quickly looked away.

Several days later, we returned to New York, where we'd planned a Christmas dinner for Lee's family. His ninety-one-year-old mother had just been diagnosed with lung cancer and was scheduled for surgery in mid-January. On Christmas Eve, I caught the nursing home virus and spent Christmas in bed. Lee carried the turkey and the rest of the food over to his mother's apartment. I was sick for the next ten days and couldn't imagine how my mother had survived the illness.

Finally, on a wintry January morning, we hired an ambulance to bring my mother home. I'd made sure to keep all the decorations in place so she could see them, but the ambulance workers brought her directly upstairs on a stretcher. I'd ordered a hospital bed and it was now in Nancy's old room.

My mother was dying, but I didn't know it then. She'd been in the process of dying in the nursing home, but I didn't know that, either. Maybe doctors and nurses are so inured to death that they think what's obvious to them is obvious to everyone. Maybe it's like the Victorian figurines or the love in my father's eyes. It's visible and invisible.

I rubbed her feet for hours. "You have such healing hands," she kept repeating. We drove to her favorite restaurant, Joe Fish, to bring back her much-loved tuna melt, but she ate only a few tiny bites. Nevertheless, I was sure she'd rebound. Nothing could keep my mother down for long. In a weak voice, she told me that the neighbors had a new beagle puppy. I think she was angling for me to write a children's story about it. I told her I loved her and that I'd see her soon. Lee's mother was being operated on for lung cancer the next morning and we needed to be back in New York.

Three days later, I received a call from Nancy telling me that she was heading to Andover. The nurse said my mother was ready for hospice. She was failing, and failing fast. I called Emily, but she told me that she and my mother had said their private good-byes the previous weekend. Lee and I raced back to Andover, but by then, my mother had lapsed into a coma.

My father held my mother's hand. Nancy's nine-year-old daughter Isabel sat across from her. She'd made her grandmother a special monogrammed pillow, which she nestled under my mother's arm. Isabel hadn't wanted to leave the room, even though Nancy was afraid it might be too upsetting for her. Later, I asked Isabel why she'd stayed. "Because I loved Nana," she said simply.

Lee and my brother-in-law Mark stood at the foot of the bed. Nancy and I sat on either side of my mother and stroked her head. I'd read that hearing is the last sense to go. I don't know if it's true, but Nancy played a CD of the Irish tenor John McCormack, whose voice sounded exactly like Bumpa's. As he sang Handel's Panis Angelicus, my mother stirred slightly, took several big breaths, and then one long exhale. "She's gone," I heard the home-care attendant say. I immediately put my ear to her chest and listened to her heart. It beat four more times, and then a half beat, and then nothing.

My father wept openly. I'd never seen him shed a tear in his life and it was heartbreaking. The priest arrived to perform the Anointing of the Sick, and afterward the men from the funeral parlor removed my mother, who was now "the body." They took her—"it"— down the stairs feetfirst. Nancy went into my mother's bedroom to find clothes for the wake.

"What about the suit Mommy wore to my wedding?" she asked.

"Mommy wore black to your wedding?"

"Yeah, what's wrong with that?"

"Oh, nothing . . . but it's perfect for a wake."

We searched the closet for shoes but could find only the New Balance sneakers. Perhaps she'd known her traveling days were over and had given most of her other shoes away. Nancy and I were frantic. My mother couldn't wear sneakers with a suit.

"We can't find shoes," Nancy told the funeral director, a sweet-faced man who projected quiet confidence.

"She doesn't need them," he said matter-of-factly.

She doesn't need *shoes*? I thought of Paul walking barefoot on the *Abbey Road* cover. Was it a ritual I didn't know about, something about entering the Kingdom of Heaven without shoes? But it was a more practical consideration. She didn't need shoes because the coffin covered the lower part of her body.

"At least she needs pantyhose," Nancy said.

"And my pillow," Isabel added.

Thirty-nine years, twenty-seven days, and three hundred and sixty-nine minutes later, we were back at St. Augustine Cemetery in the snow. Except for the green carpet leading to the gravesite, practically everything was white—the flowers atop the casket, the trees glistening in the sun, the tops of the headstones, each a different size and shape. In another context and setting, my mother would have said, "It's a winter wonderland."

The priest recited prayers over the coffin. I remember the sprinkling of holy water, the sign of the cross, the phrase "Let perpetual light shine upon her." I remember Warren and Woody's sympathetic eyes; my father in the car too frail to make it up the hill; Lee's hand touching my back; Nancy fighting back tears; Emily and her family opposite me. When it was over, we all walked back down the hill, Isabel in heels for the first time. They were black satin dotted with rhinestones and made her look very grown up.

"Isn't she a little young for heels?" I whispered to Nancy.

"They're better than the leopard combat boots she wanted to wear," she said. "She's become totally shoe crazy."

Despite the setting, despite everything, we had to laugh.

Inside the funeral car, I told Isabel how much I liked her shoes. She smiled for the first time in days. "Yeah," she said. "They're totally awesome."

17

Pilgrim's Progress

A month after my mother died, my father's last sibling passed away at ninety-nine. "Now I'm the only one left," my father said. The house, which had once buzzed with my mother's high energy, was heavy with sadness. My father spent his days sitting in his blue chair reading the newspapers, but it wasn't the same. Though he'd always prized his solitude, it was different knowing my mother wasn't going to pop into the room at any moment to announce she was heading off to return another pair of shoes.

My mother had been right about finding "kind" people when you needed them. My father's home-care attendant, a lovely woman from Ghana, had recently lost her own mother. She was attentive to my father but knew when to leave him alone. There was Jack, who lived in the house that once marked the bus stop where in ninth grade I debuted my ghillies. His wife of thirty-five years had recently died of cancer, and although he was my age, he and my father bonded, two widowers from different generations but with something profound in common. He stopped by every day to say hello and trade *The Boston Globe* for the *Eagle-Tribune*. There was Klara, who headed the church's outreach program, and who gave him communion each week and then sat and talked to him.

And then there was Joan, the nurse who'd assisted in my delivery. Joan remembered my father from his college days when he used to frequent her husband's restaurant in Andover. Now in her mid-eighties, she was blond, blue-eyed, and radiantly beautiful, with a soothing presence. She said that when I was born, my mother treated me like a fragile little doll. "I think she was horrified when she saw the way Barbara and I were tossing you around in the hospital," she recalled. Barbara was the other delivery nurse and Joan's best friend.

No one fed the birds anymore and the white squirrels, looking for more hospitable backyards, disappeared. When I returned for Easter, I noticed that my mother's garden was overgrown with weeds. The window boxes were empty. I immediately went to the garden shop and bought flowers, planting bright petunias interspersed with ivy. I filled the bird feeder, hoping the white squirrels would return, but none of it mattered to my father.

Over the years, I'd related to Jane Fonda's struggle to have a relationship with her own distant father. Every time I watched *On Golden Pond* I'd dissolve into tears when Fonda's character tries to earn her father's approval by doing the backflip. Everyone knew that Chelsea and Norman were really stand-ins for Jane and Henry Fonda. I'd always dreamed of an *On Golden Pond* moment but had no idea how it would take shape, or if it would even happen. Six months before my mother died, Lee and I were were getting ready to drive back to New York when my father casually said, "Take the photo albums."

My mother wasn't happy. "I like looking at them," she said, although I'd noticed that she'd begun ripping out unflattering pictures of herself. "Go on, take them," my father insisted. I raced upstairs and grabbed the five albums. I understood how much they meant to him and appreciated all the time he'd put into them. They were his "books," a visual diary of our family, and he was entrusting them to me. Whether or not he realized it, I also think he was acknowledging that the story he'd labored over, the story of our family, was coming to a close.

Since then, we had smaller Golden Pond moments. He was fitted with new top-of-the-line hearing aids, which made a huge improvement. It allowed us to talk on the phone, though our conversations were mainly about finances. He was worried about the high cost of twenty-four-hour care and how fast he'd deplete his savings. In 1988, Shawmut Bank had acquired the Arlington Trust Company and the two entities became part of Bank of America, one of the biggest offenders in the subprime mortgage scandal. For someone who'd spent the majority of his career carefully screening people for mortgages, it was ironic that my father's Bank of America stock would take a hit due to such irresponsible practices.

The table next to his blue reading chair was piled high with bills and bank statements, all neatly organized and wrapped in elastic bands. He kept his will and other important documents in a metal lockbox at the foot of his chair, along with a white three-ring binder in which he'd laid out in meticulous detail all the steps my mother needed to take in the event of his death. He'd assumed he'd be the first to go. He'd even written his own obituary, telling Nancy to make sure I didn't add any unnecessary flourishes.

Once when Nancy was visiting, he brought up the idea of going into a nursing home. "But don't you want to stay at home?" she asked.

"What's a home?" he responded.

When he'd lost his mother as a young boy, he'd also lost his home. He'd lived in a convent, a boarding school, and a series of Army barracks. When he found my mother, he'd found a home, but without her, he felt he had none.

At the end of July, he fell in the bathroom, and when he was taken to the emergency room, he was diagnosed with pneumonia. It eventually cleared up, but he'd hurt his ankle and knees, which made walking even more difficult. In a repeat of what happened to my mother, he went from the hospital into a nursing home for rehab. This time I made sure to select a different one. It was part of a retirement complex, where people fifty-five and older can buy a condo and then transition into assisted living and the nursing home. The director of admissions turned out to be a former colleague of Nancy's. They had a private room in the rehab section where, if he decided to stay, he could remain permanently. It was bright and cheery and on the first floor.

Before Lee and I moved him from the hospital, we stopped by the house to pick up his mail. As we drove down my old street, I commented that it would be one of the few times I'd be going into the house without one of my parents greeting me. We pulled into the driveway and there, by the front steps, was one of the white squirrels.

"I think it's your mother," Lee said.

"And she's telling me to write a children's story."

I thought I'd feel sad entering the house, but it was a beautiful sunny day, the living room infused with light, the flowers still blooming in the window boxes. I'd called the landscapers and they'd done extensive cutting and weeding. It felt like a home, not necessarily mine anymore, and indeed, I'd left it decades ago, but a place still filled with love.

Afterward, we went to the nursing home, which is in North Andover, on thirty-seven acres of rolling hills and meadows. My father's room has a lovely view, where he can watch the seasons change. I asked him if he wanted me to bring over a few family photographs to tack on the bulletin board or place on his bureau, but he said no. At first I was offended, but then I realized it was too painful for him. I also imagined bringing the little porcelain boy, who'd accompanied him everywhere on his journey, but I couldn't bring the little boy without the matching little girl, and the little girl was gone. When we said good-bye, he told me, "I don't know what I'd do without you." I cried most of the way back to New York.

✿

With everything that had happened with both our families, Lee and I hadn't taken time off in a year and a half, and we were both exhausted. At the end of August, we decided to go to Tuscany. Our hotel was in the tiny southern village of Palazzetto, near the slightly larger Chiusdino. The thirteenth-century stone-clad villa overlooked the Serena Valley and had once served as a stopping-off point for medieval pilgrims walking the Via Francigena, which ran from Canterbury, through France and Switzerland, and finally to Rome. The hotel's small spa, located in a stone building, had once served as the bakery where the pilgrims would be given bread before heading to the nearby Abbey of San Galgano.

After resting for a day, we took off to the abbey, part of a ruined thirteenth-century Cistercian monastery that was named after Saint Galgano. According to legend, he'd seen a vision of Jesus, Mary, and the Apostles, who told him to renounce his materialistic ways. He replied that it would be easier to split a rock with a sword. Embedded in a stone, the sword is on display in a circular church above the abbey. For years it had been considered a hoax, but recent metal-dating tests confirmed the sword's medieval origins. Many believe it was the inspiration for the Arthurian legends, but even if it wasn't, the abbey and church are beautiful.

We continued to walk, creating our own pilgrim's path. We climbed up and down cobbled medieval streets, dropping in at small churches with disappearing frescos, eating mozzarella and tomato panini in outdoor restaurants with views of clock towers and fortresses and remnants of Etruscan walls. At night, we fell into bed exhausted, only to start walking again the next day. I wore comfortable navy sneakers with heavily cushioned inserts. I was no longer thinking about shoes but about the pure joy of walking.

We ended the trip in Rome, where our hotel was preparing for a big Middle Eastern wedding. In the lobby, I encountered a group of women dressed in traditional head scarves and long black abayas. Apparently they, too, wanted to be comfortable as they walked the city streets. Peeking out from beneath their robes were identical Jimmy Choo sequined sneakers.

❧

After we returned to New York, we went to visit my father, whose rehab period was about to end. We discussed bringing him home, but he feared that even with twenty-four-hour care he might take a bad fall, and there were too many medical complications. I think he also enjoyed the activity. He made friends with the nurses and attendants, and Jack and Joan dropped by at least once a week. One of Joan's close friends happened to be in the room across from my father's.

Though she slept much of the day, when she woke up, she and my father waved at each other. It comforted him.

That night we stayed in the house, in the room where my mother died. It felt surprisingly peaceful. The next morning, I gathered some of my old things to bring back to New York. At the beginning of the summer, I'd spotted a pair of white oxfords that I liked but were too expensive. By July, they were half-price, so I bought them. As I walked from room to room, I heard my mother's voice telling me, "White *shoes? Are you crazy?*" But white was the color of my "first love," Mary Janes. White was the color of the squirrels. It was the color of the snow that fell during weddings and funerals and births. And now it was the color of the shoes I wore when I said good-bye to the house. Though I knew I'd be returning, it felt like the final walk-through.

The big surprise was that my mother hadn't "pitched and chucked" everything after all. In fact, she'd been downright sentimental. She'd kept my Shirley Temple doll, with the unraveled ringlets; all my letters from London; every report card and school paper and magazine article that carried my byline. Hidden away on the top shelf of her closet was a pair of brand-new shoes. A former neighbor asked if she could have them. She'd gone with my mother to buy them, and knowing how frustrating that must have been, I happily gave them to her. I also found the gold mesh bag my mother had carried to cocktail parties fifty years earlier. Inside was a handkerchief that still smelled of My Sin. Inhaling the scent, I immediately pictured her black stilettos. Next to the purse was my baby book covered in pink satin. I slipped it into my overnight bag to bring back with me to New York.

When Lee and I left the house, the white squirrels were scampering in the backyard. "I'd like to have the bird feeder," Lee said. "We could put it right in front of our kitchen window and look at the birds just as your mother did."

"So we'll become bird-watchers in our old age?"

He laughed. "At least we'll have something in common."

✧

I didn't look at the baby album for several weeks. I felt it would make me too sad. When I finally opened it, I had to smile. Glued to the first page was a birth announcement that read JUST ARRIVED TO FILL THESE SHOES. . . . There was a picture of a pair of blue baby shoes with pink laces on the front. On the opposite page, my mother had written down my birth date, the hour of my birth, my weight, and the names of the delivery nurses, including Joan, who was then Miss Hardy, and another nurse, Miss Winters.

My mother noted that I'd made my first attempt at crawling upstairs at ten months. At a year, I took four steps and "walked soon after." Lacking my father's focus, my mother worked on the book intermittently, and *Patricia's Baby Album* contained mostly blank pages. She'd always wanted me to write a children's story, so perhaps she'd left it up to me to finish it.

A few days later, flipping through the book again, my eye stopped at the name of the second delivery nurse. I had a hunch and called my father.

"Remember the nurse who helped deliver me?" I asked.

"Sure, Joan."

"No, the other one. Miss Winters."

"Oh, that's Barbara. She's the one across the hall. I'm waving to her now."

What were the odds that the two women who were present at my birth would be close to my father as he neared the end of his life? It almost made me believe in angels.

When I looked at the baby album again, I noticed something else. My mother had been inconsistent about keeping up with my various childhood milestones, but in her random jottings, she'd seen the future:

"Patricia loves books."

"She loves asking questions."

"She loves wearing my shoes."

Epilogue

The other day, I bumped into my friend Nancy, who lives in my building and is a 9½ narrow too. Over the years, we've discussed our favorite topics: shoes and mothers. Now that we've grown older and traded high heels for lower ones, we've also come to view our mothers from a different perspective. We've gone from complaining about them, to accepting their foibles, to outright admiration for their grit and determination. We always loved them; it took time and maturity to walk in their shoes.

Nancy told me that her mother, who is eighty-nine and lives in Florida, recently suffered a series of unexplained falls. Up until then, she'd enjoyed an active life but is now housebound. "I just got off the phone with my sister," she said. "She was driving to the Goodwill to donate my mother's shoes! I told her to turn the car around. 'Take away her shoes,' I said, 'and you take away her hope.'"

I suddenly thought of an Emily Dickinson poem that I'd memorized in grade school. It's about the endurance of a bird's song through dark times. I've always loved the quirky opening line: "Hope is the thing with feathers." Hope, I've discovered, is also the thing with bows and rhinestones and studs, with kitten heels and platforms, red soles and beige. Hope is the reason I'm back at Bergdorf Goodman in search of a pair of knee-high boots to replace the ones I wore to my mother's funeral.

Today, the shoe department isn't offering champagne but it's still packed with shoppers. Women in all shapes and sizes are walking up and down in every conceivable type of shoe. I stand at the entrance and watch the colorful parade, almost expecting confetti to rain down from the ceiling. As the women gaze at their reflections in the full-length mirrors, they rotate their feet to make sure a particular style flatters their legs. If they're wearing pants, they roll them up. If they're wearing dresses or skirts, they sometimes twirl around to view the shoes in motion. Sometimes they just stare, as if creating stories in their heads. No matter their ages, they're like children playing dress-up. These women are not buying shoes to please men. They're buying shoes to please themselves.

As I try on a variety of boots, in black and gray, suede and calfskin, I see the gumball machine and the fluoroscope, the marabou mules and Beatle boots. I think of my mother, and I'd love to go back in time if only for an hour or two. I find myself getting teary, so I thank the salesman and take the bus home. A few hours later, I go online and find the perfect boots in snakeskin and suede. They have a two-inch block heel, a rounded toe, and a narrow profile. With their multiple textures, they remind me of the 1970s, which really wasn't my fashion decade, but maybe it will be now. Picturing myself in the boots, I hear my mother say, "*Snakeskin? Are you crazy?*" And then I hear the flutter of wings, and I know that hope, in 9½ narrow, is on its way.

Acknowledgments

I'd like to thank my father for everything, my sister Nancy for her high spirits and knotted hair, and my niece Isabel for being such a joy. A special thank-you to Clarice Kestenbaum, whose shoes no one could possibly fill.

I am lucky to have kept the same incredible friends for decades. My deepest gratitude goes to Woody for being the best pal a girl could ever have, and to Warren, who's so vain he probably thinks this book is about him. I adore you both (in equal measure). I'd also like to thank Ira Fogel and Pamela Fogel for entrusting me with Steffi's story. I miss her every day. Thanks to Ira Resnick, Jamie and Jenny Delson, Glynnis O'Connor, James Danziger, Jack Henry, Suzanne Eagle, Richard Story, Jennifer Crandall, and Robin Sherman. A special thanks goes to Elaine Altholz, who put this book in motion, Nancy Cromer Grayson, who provided the ending, and to Marie Colantoni Pechet for her inspiring blog.

A big thank-you to my incredibly supportive editor, Lauren Marino, and to her energetic team at Gotham. I am indeed fortunate to have the wonderful Emma Sweeney as my agent.

To my mother-in-law, Dorothy Stern, all I can say is please keep your amazing pea soup coming. As for my husband, Lee, thanks for finally admitting that the mysterious steamer trunk in our storage bin contains some of the Puma sneakers I thought you'd given away. And no, I don't believe you held on to the red patent-leather ones to commemorate our first date. Still, I love you. Thanks for walking beside me.